SCRUM

The Ultimate Guide for Beginners to Learn Scrum

HENRY GEORGE

TABLE OF CONTENTS

Introduction

Scrum is defined as a framework that enhances teamwork. It is a kind of training for those who work in groups and it encourages learning through problem-solving. Teams can overcome real project obstacles while working on concrete problems and finding solutions. Scrum empowers self-organization and constant improvement. Scrum is usually used in software development. The most frequent teams that use its principles are those who work in big companies and on big projects. Still, Scrum lessons can be used in any kind of teamwork. This is the reason why Scrum has become frequently applied to many corporations and smaller firms. This framework represents an ideal way of working for project managers and it is agile. Additionally, Scrum has numerous tools and features that are necessary for a successful task. It offers described roles, tools and meetings that you need in order to get a structured and efficient team.

Chapter 1

Definition of Scrum and
Its First Appearance

We can say that the accepted attitude about system development is that these processes are highly understood. The philosophy behind this is that every approach can and should be planned. Every act can be calculated, structured and efficiently implemented. Still, the practice says otherwise. On the other hand, the basic belief behind Scrum is that the system is unpredictable and that development is complicated. That is why Scrum is generally based on their definition of the system on overall progression rather than a predictable process. According to Scrum, the development of the system is a set of activities that are loose. The development combines workable techniques that we know of and tools that can be used by development teams. Furthermore, these tools are devised by teams to build the desired systems. Scrum suggests that loose activities disable precise management. That is why teams need to be ready to take some amount of risk. This being said, Scrum represents a kind of enhancement for development cycles that are oriented on objects.

Practices that are considered to be the best of Scrum have evolved over the decades. They have also changed. In early papers, Scrum was simplified and some companies like Patient Keeper didn't have the closing phase of the project at the end of the 20th century. At first, Scrum had to pass many tests in order to achieve acceptance. These tests along with training and other documentation were all a part of the so-called Sprint which is one of the sections in Scrum. Afterward, the Scrum framework was produced and sold to many companies. At that moment, Scrum's demo became an advanced framework with a large network of users. Some say that it became a live system that implemented advanced Sprint variations. Advanced Scrum principles and practices have been put into one course. This course is called the Certified Scrum Master and it is one of the core training tools. It was developed by the first team in Easel Corporation that ever used this framework. Certified Scrum Master became official in 1993. It consists of several categories such as monthly iterations, sprints, meetings with three questions daily, etc. This first Scrum Master not only had additional backlogs and impediments, but it also implemented engineering principles of eXtreme Programming a few years before well known Kent Becks' codified XP.

The first official paper on Scrum was written in 1995 by Jeff Sutherland. He was one of the lecturers at OOPSLA conferences. Sutherland was organizing a series of workshops about Business Object design, and he was the main lecturer on Ken Schwaber's implementations of those designs between 1995 and 2000. The first paper about Scrum was published for the OOPSLA'95 annual conference. Jeff Sutherland had the opportunity to observe how the first Scrum works. Later, he set the basic principles for its operations. Even now, Sutherlands' writing remains one of the most important and most popular papers from OOPSLA workshops. The original paper about Scrum can be found on Jeff Sutherlands' website: http://jeffsutherland.com/Scrum. The complex theory of Scrum is introduced together with the difference between the empirical process and prediction. This distinction is important because business enterprises are complex. They represent adaptive systems, and so are the software programs that run them. Some experts compare business enterprises to biological systems. Complexity and speed of change and adaptations are similar. It's like an evolution of a live system. However, artificial existence is more flexible and faster to adapt. Its flexibility increases proportionally with chaos. We need empirical processes to prevent and control chaotic and unwanted behavior. Sutherland believes that this is the essence of Scrum. The leader of this first empirical process in real Scrum practice was Mike Beedle. He set elaboration and organization patterns along with the Jeff Sutherland – the author of the paper, and Ken Schwaber

Additional information about Scrum's core principles was described in the later papers of Mike Beedle and Ken Schwaber. These papers are called ''Agile Development with Scrum.' Jeff Sutherland's contributions were added in a volume called ''Agile Can Scale: Inventing and Reinventing Scrum in Five Companies'' In the last 15 years, Ken Schwaber worked as a Scrum consultant in several companies, while Sutherland was conducting research in at least five. The biggest business enterprises he used for his Scrum research are IDX, Easel, Patient Keeper, VMARK and Individual. Schwaber and Sutherland continued testing and evolving Scrum together over the years. One of the things that they were interested in the most was the hyper-production of teams. This happened with the first Scrum too. They believed that hyper-productivity is connected to the structure of deployment in Scrum teams. It also depends on the maturity of the stages that are implemented in the team structure.

Chapter 2

The Development
Process of the Scrum

In this chapter, we will also talk about the development process of Scrum. This process is compared to a black box for system development. The complex theory of this black box is related to the approach of increased flexibility. The purpose is to be able to deal with complex production in systems that are highly responsive and adaptable. Responsiveness is connected to both basic and additional requirements of the software. Many approaches describe the improvement of the development process, and many of them have been already implemented. However, all of these attempts failed in producing significant improvements.

One of the implementers, named Grady Booch, wrote that a condition without production improvements is called a software crisis. Still, he thinks that these kinds of setbacks are normal. Many industrial concepts of process control are used to improve systems in development in Scrum. The industrial process is defined theoretically or empirically. The first definition is also called a full definition while the empirical one is described through the comparison with the black box. It is said that there can be unpredictable results if we treat the empirical industrial process as a fully defined one.

A large amount of systems in the development process are treated as fully defined even though they are often defined just partially. As we already explained, unpredictable results can be expected from this kind of control. If we observe Scrum, we will see that it uses the approach of the black box. Still, in Scrum, this black box is controlled and it controls all other segments of the system.

For example, Scrum's first highly productive performance of new product development was used on small teams in companies such as Fuji-Xerox, Honda, Canon, Nonaka 3, Epson, 3M, etc. Contrarily, a slightly adjusted Scrum was used on Borland's software development project. This was the most productive C++ project that was ever seen at the time. In recent years, companies such as SmallTalk and Sutherland set more refined versions of Scrum and they are using them for their development project called Schwaberto Delphi. Scrum framework is used by successful companies. It works like a leading-edge for big software enterprises. Nevertheless, Scrum principles can be applied to other organizations. As long as their purpose is to realize what their objectives are, and they are ready to use object-oriented tools, Scrum applies to a high rate for success.

Systems' development new approach uses two kinds of process management. The first one is fully defined process management, and the other is the so-called black box. This approach is also known as Scram methodology. This term was introduced in project development in Nonaka and Takeuchi in 1986. Firstly, Scrum was used in rugby. It involved formations that were tight and that were binding specified positions whenever the ''Scrumdown'' was called. We already mentioned that Scrum can be observed as an enhancement. This is mostly because it positively affects incremental and iterative approaches. These properties of Scrum, along with the object-oriented features, were first described by Mr. Pittman. Booch took these papers and expanded them later on.

Some of the Scrum's categories are similarly outlined as Graham indicated. This mostly refers to the role of the project staff. Still, Scrum differently organizes teams and manages them in another way. The methodology of Scrum is based on the enhancement, management, and maintenance of a system. This also refers to production prototypes. Scrum works on a premise that code and design already exist. This is usually true for virtual development and it is due to the existence of the class libraries. It is only after this assumed existence is implemented that Scrum will address the efforts of systems that are legacies or just re-engineered already existent systems.

Strategic variables

When it comes to product releases of software, several variables influence the strategy:

- Current enhancement based on customer requirements

- The time frame that you need to be competitive. This is also called a ''time pressure'' variable, and it refers to the amount of time you need to gain competitiveness.

- Looking at the competition – teams must be aware of the work of competition and find a way to do better.

- Teams need to be mindful of the quality of the product. They need to calculate quality that will cover other variables.

- What is the vision for the product? Teams must think about the changes that need to be made to fulfill the best vision of the system.

- What are your resources? Funding is one of the most important aspects of any project. It defines the conditions and the number of staff that you can acquire for system development. It is especially important for enhancing product release.

Keep in mind that these variables can change. Still, if you want to implement a successful methodology, you must take variables into consideration. They can evolve during the project or they can set you back if you are not careful enough.

Situation Systems nowadays have a very complicated environment. That is why the development system itself can be complicated. Complexity can come from two sources: one is the target environment, and the other one is the development environment. A good example of this can be air traffic control systems. At first, there was no need to take airline deregulation or three-tier client-server into consideration. Still, there were changes in the environment and in technical aspects of air traffic. These are all occurrences that influence the functioning of the system and they had to be taken into account when the system was later built.

Environmental variables

Environmental variables are significant for Scrum methodology. They include:

- Professionals who are skilled and available. If you use newer technology, there is a bigger chance that the number of

- skilled professionals is smaller. The numbers are even smaller when it comes to software tools and domains.

- You need to establish if the technology you want to implement is stable. New technologies can be unstable because they haven't had the chance to pass the test of time. They also need more add-ons for balancing and manual synchronizations.

- Other variables that connect to the stability of your project are the tools and their power. There are risks in using the newest and more powerful tools. It can also mean that there aren't many professionals skilled enough to implement them.

- How effective your methods are? This variable depends on the versions of control you want for your project, it depends on modeling that you will use. Testing and design also affect this feature. The overall results will depend on the efficiency and effectiveness of this variable.

- Do you have professionals in the area of domain expertise? Are they capable of working in different domains, and do they include technology and business ones?

- What are the new features of your project? In what way will they benefit the functionality?

- Do you use flexible approaches? Is your methodology based on rigid terms with detailed instructions or is it adaptable

- Your team needs to be aware of the competition and their work during the project. Is there any new feature that they will announce too?

- The time frame and funding are of the utmost importance. You need to be aware of the overall amount of time that was given to you and compare it with the progress of the project. Financing should be also calculated in a time frame. Keep track of the amount of money available for the development.

- Additional factors that can influence the whole process. Sometimes unpredicted events can happen with staff members for example. That is why you need to be able to respond quickly. One of the other variables that you might need to consider is a reorganization.

Variables represent a complex part of Scrum, and it is due to their overall function. Complexity is defined as a function of environmental variables plus variables of the target environment in the development system. Furthermore, variables tend to change during the project. If the project is complicated, complexity will increase. That is why you need to have proper ways to control response risks and ongoing assessments.

Model making problems

Problems that appeared in attempts to make models for development processes are:

- The fact that a large number of these processes are not controlled. If you don't define inputs and outputs for your project, there can't be any precision during the process of transformation. This way you are not able to define quality control. The same thing happens if you have just a loose definition for your inputs and outputs. A good example of this is any testing process.

- Sometimes there are unknown numbers of processes in development that are unidentified. This means that they are uncontrollable. In this case, you need to have detailed processes that will ensure that there is adequate content for each particular model. If the content is relevant and logical, it will increase the possibility of making a physical model and enable a successful process.

- Environmental requirements need to be considered at the beginning of the project. Once the environmental inputs have been implemented, complex management actions can start.

Chapter 3

Detailed Methodologies

The reason why too detailed methodology approaches haven't been successful in development process is that they are not defined completely. If you act like these processes are predictable, you won't be prepared for unpredictable situations and results.

Several detailed methodologies are based on current methods of development. In the next paragraphs, we will discuss the Waterfall methodology, which is one of the first detailed and defined methodologies for system development. We will also talk about Spiral and Iterative methodologies. Finally, we will discuss more details about the functioning and phases of Scrum.

Waterfall and Spiral Methodology

The waterfall approach works on the premise that undefined processes exist and they need to be controlled. Still, this methodology has a linear nature and that is why it has some shortcomings. For example, Waterfall doesn't offer any solution for unexpected outputs. The spiral methodology created by Barry Boehm addressed this issue later. Contrarily, in each of Waterfall phases, there is an end caused by the risk of assessment or activities that suggest making prototypes.

The Spiral methodology is based on the ''layers'' and it predicts more aspects and variables in system development processes. For example, unlike Waterfall, Spiral methodology allows the user to try the prototype. It lets you estimate if the project is on the right path. This way you can see, firsthand, if the project needs to be returned to some of the prior phases. You can also determine if the project is successful or unsuccessful and end it. Even though Spiral principles give more insight into the development than the Waterfall method, the phases of projects still have linear construction. This means that if your requirement is designed, you have to do only design in that phase. If it is coding, you only have to do coding, and so forth. Every process is strictly defined and explained in detail without any room for flexibility.

Iterative Methodology

The Iterative methodology is an improvement on the first two. Iterations have phases that are standard for Waterfall phases; still, iterations address only one set of functionalities. Deliverables of the project are divided into subsystems and ordered by priority. The interface is clear and defined for subsystems individually.

This methodology is useful to test the subsystem's technology and its feasibility. The advantage is that this can be done in some of the initial phases. As the project advances, iterations can be used to get additional resources, and it can speed up the delivery of the project. Iterative methodology means that you will have good control over your costs and improves the system of delivery and flexibility. Yet, there are some of the processes in the Iterative approach that retained its linear definition.

Scrum Methodology

As we already explained in the previous paragraphs, the system development process is not simple. It has many unpredictable variables; therefore its complexity requires flexible solutions. The evolution of technology showed that to have a successful project one has to work with full flexibility. This also means that you need to be prepared to be completely exposed to environmental changes. In this era, it is useless to try to make your environment less complex and to try to avoid chaos. Working teams have to embrace an approach that helps them adapt to excessive changes and predict efficient solutions that are not always too precise.

It is already clear that every system development happens in circumstances that can change rapidly. This also means that even producing systems based on existent technologies under chaotic and diverse variables has to be flexible.

The team needs to be ready to work under the pressure of chaotic conditions and maintain order. Although this requires flexibility and many unknown areas, it also increases competitiveness and brings more efficient production. The complexity theory introduced by Langton was based on a modeled effect that was used in computer simulations. This simulation was later recognized as one of the fundamental discoveries that explained the principles of complexity in system developing processes. One of the most important factors in estimating the probability of success is the methodology that is used on the project. It was proven that the methodologies that promote flexible approaches have a higher degree of success and better responsiveness on changes in variables.

Waterfall, Spiral and Iterative methodology were used for software development in companies such as Easel, ADM and VMARK, and it reflected their experiences. These companies were ready to take a risk and have built the most successful software of the moment. In this context, they increased the impact of their products and changed the meaning of deliverables by including environmental factors.

Scrum methodology defines all these processes as undefined completely. The purpose of the Scrum is to use mechanisms that will effectively improve flexibility and control. The main distinction between fully defined approaches such as Waterfall or Spiral and Scrum is that Scrum has a hypothesis that Sprint is unpredictable in terms of analysis or design. That is why Scrum has a special focus on risk control and management of unpredictable variables. The overall goal of Scrum is to enhance responsiveness and increases the results during the system development process.

Some of the main characteristics of the Scrum methodology are:

- The only fully defined processes are the first phase called planning, and the last phase called the closure. All of the processes during these two phases need to have clear inputs and outputs. Scrum uses some of the iterations in the planning part which gives it a linear flow.

- The sprint category that we mentioned multiple times is actually an empirical phase. This is where Scrum's undefined premises are compared with the black box. These uncontrollable processes need to have external mechanisms of control. Scrum predicts this with the sections such as risk management for iterations individually during the Sprint.

That is how a team can achieve maximum flexibility and reduce chaos.

- Sprint can have multiple parts and it isn't linear. It is part of the Scrum approach which is the most flexible one. Teams can use the knowledge that is explicit if they can, but if that's not the case, tactical knowledge can be used. Tactical knowledge means that the team builds experience and looks for solutions through tests and errors. The purpose of the Sprint phase is to help the final product evolve to its maximum.

- In Scrum, environmental variables can influence the project until the Closure. It also enables the change of deliverables during the whole first phase and Sprint. Variables can change during these two sections and they include time frame, resources, environmental changes and quality of the product.

- •Last but not least; Scrum is different because it allows the teams to determine the deliverables following the environmental requirements.

One of the Scrum Phase divisions

Phases of the scrum can be divided into groups. The first group is the **Pregame**. It consists of planning that needs to provide a definition of a planned release. This definition has to be based on backlog knowledge and to have an estimated cost and schedule. If the team wants to develop a completely new system, they need to provide a concept and analysis of their product in this phase.

Architecture is also in this group. It means that the team needs to provide the concept for a design for their backlog items. They also need to explain how they will implement this design.

The second group is the **Game**. This group includes Sprints for development. The team needs to determine the functionality of their new release. They need to include environmental variables and to predict flexible ways to increase their responsiveness in terms of quality of their product, requirements of their product, time frame for their deliverables. They need to have a flexible plan for costs and funding during the system development phase and to include competition and its impact on the productivity of the team. There have to be multiple Sprints during this phase to evolve the system's deliverables.

The third group is called **Postgame**. In this phase, teams that implement Scrum approach enter the Closure. This means that the teams finished all previous stages successfully and that they are ready to prepare for the final release of their product. Once the management team sees that the variables have been successfully resolved they will declare the project as closed. Additional tasks for the Closure are preparation for integrating the product and necessary adjustments for general release. Scrum includes final tests before releasing the product. It also includes all necessary paperwork like financial reports, product licenses, patent rights, etc. This phase also covers user manuals, final system checks, documentation for training, and so forth. One of the significant aspects of Post Game is that the team needs to prepare a marketing campaign that will launch their final product.

Avoiding chaos due to many unpredictable factors is one of the strongest features of Scrum methodology. Mature and well-structured management is necessary to empower this kind of approach. Scrum is used to provide external control for undefined inputs and outputs. The reason why Scrum is so popular is that it enables teams to have a good insight into their tasks and helps them to increase their productivity and quality of the whole system development process. In the end, successful Scrum implementation means that your product is ready to be on the market.

Chapter 4

Systems of Control in Scrum

As we previously mentioned, Scrum uses several methods to provide external control in the process of system development. These controls are:

- A backlog is a form of control in which we need to address the functionality of the product and its requirements that haven't been defined right in the current description of the project release. This means that in the backlog, Scrum deals with enhancements asked for by customers and bugs or defects of the product. It also addresses upgrades in terms of technology and competitiveness of the product.

- In the phase of release or enhancement, Scrum uses backlog items. These items are improved in the release phase of the product using the info that teams gathered on variables such as quality, time and strength of competition.

- Components of every project use packet as another form of external control. If the packets are used, the product changes, following the backlog items and a new release plan.

- One of the most frequently used forms of external control in Scrum is change. It is predicted that changes must happen to every packet if they want to implement enhancements of the backlog items.

- In many cases, we meet with problems during the development processes. But if we want to have a successful implementation of the changes, we must resolve any technical problems that might occur.

- Every system in the developing process is faced with risks. Risks can seriously affect the project and its success. That is why is necessary to be prepared and to be responsive in this stage. Risk assessment can affect every other phase and it can totally change the course of the project.

- Teams are always required to provide solutions to these risks and problems. Sometimes solutions to certain risks or problem-solving lead to big changes in the product release phase.

- Teams must also be prepared to face issues that are not described in any previous method of control. There can be some overall project issues in different phases of Scrum. These issues are usually used by management to properly manage backlog items. On the other hand, teams use them to find solutions and make changes. However, management and the teams can't control risks or solutions individually. They need to work together if they want to increase their productivity. Also, these mechanisms of control are changeable. They are reviewed in every Sprint meeting when the whole team discuss, modifies and reconciles them.

Deliverables in Scrum

The product that is delivered at the end of the development process is flexible. The content of this product depends on many variables, especially the environmental ones. As it was already mentioned, some of these variables are funding, time frame, work of the competition and functionality of the product itself. When we talk about determinants for our deliverables, we need to consider the intelligence of the market. We also need to include the contacts of our customers and the skills of our developers. In the phase of development, many changes occur. These changes or adjustments are frequent for the products. They represent the team's answer to environmental variables. Keep in mind that in Scrum, you can determine deliverables in any stage of the project.

Project Team in Scrum

The project team in Scrum is a team of developers who work full time on the product. The project team also includes external parties which will be affected by the release of that new product. External parties are customers and marketing sales. When it comes to traditional processes of product release, groups that are not developers are not included in the system development process because there is a possibility of making the project too much complicated. There is also a possibility of strong interference that is not necessary or useful for the project. On the other hand, Scrum allows external groups to be involved even though it is a controlled involvement set in short time intervals. According to the Scrum approach, this kind of feedback will increase the results of the project release. It is an object-oriented tool that helps developers address the right behaviors of the product and have a clear interface.

Scrum strategies have many resemblances with the strategies of the sport called Rugby. Scrum, the same as Rugby uses the environment (in Rugby it in the field) to set the context of their strategies. This also helps them establish their system of external controls (we compare it to the rules of Rugby). Also, Scrum uses its first cycle to move its product (ball) forward in the game (or in this case the system development process). Additionally, just like Rugby evolved because some soccer rules were broken, the Scrum used the same principle to evolve. They both succeeded to adapt to the changes in the environment. In the end, the game will not end as long as there are changes in their surroundings (in Scrum, this refers to the needs of the business, time frame, work of the competition and overall functionality of the product).

Scrum Methodology and its advantages

Unlike the traditional development methodologies, Scrum is not designed to respond to environmental changes only at the beginning of the cycle of enhancements. It isn't designed to respond to just too unpredictable external factors. These approaches that are more recent, like Boehm spiral methodology for example still have some limitations. This is mostly because they are not flexible enough to be responsive to all variables that can change once when the project starts. Contrarily, Scrum represents a methodology that is flexible during the whole project, in all its stages. It is a framework designed to provide mechanisms that externally control product planning and its release. Scrum manages aspects such as risk assessment, environmental variables, etc, and all other issues that can happen during the progress of the project. With this flexibility, the team can change the project at any time and create deliverables that will evolve and become more suitable for release. It enables the product to find a better place on the market.

Scrum helps developers to find solutions for many different problems or adjustments that need to be done through the whole system development process. It enables them to learn and to build experience in predicting the outcomes of environmental changes and create an appropriate response to those changes. This has an even better result if the team is small and collaborative. Scrum also has an environmental training mode that is available to all parties involved with the project. The core principle of Scrum methodology is object-oriented technology. According to Scrum's philosophy, objects that are actually features of the product already offer their own environment that is discrete but also manageable. Code which has many intertwined interfaces during the procedures doesn't work well in Scrum. However, Scrum can be applied to these procedural developing systems selectively. It can be used only in sections that offer data orientation which is strong, and it can be applied only on clear interfaces.

Scrum Project

We can estimate a Scrum projects trough some of the standard criteria for estimation. Still, when it comes to Scrum methodology, the recommendation is to double this estimation in terms of productivity. Rationally, all this is possible to determine only for the project to start. The real time frame and overall cost of the project are the things that can change through the course of the project, and they depend on variables and their changeability. Scrum is considered to have both of the most important aspects of project estimation. These aspects are acceleration and velocity in all stages of the system development process. These two criteria can be predicted by their delivered functions, or the estimation can be done observing the backlog items that have completed. In these terms, we will see that the acceleration and velocity of the project are lower in the beginning since the overall infrastructure of the system is yet to be built or modified. Also, as we put the basic function of the project into objects, the acceleration will rise. Still, acceleration will decrease when a team needs to develop new metrics for empirical processes. In this case, the velocity is high and remains sustainable until the development of the required metrics is finished.

Chapter 5

Methodologies of
the System Development

Firstly, we need to describe a development system in terms of its definition and empirical properties. The system's development empirical attribute is defined as ''the act of creating a logical construct that is implemented as logic and data on computers.'' This construct is made of logical processes of combined inputs and outputs that are used in both macro and microenvironments. This means that this process can refer to the whole construction or just to intermediate steps that are the most important in that same construction. The implemented system is a system of the whole. When the system is built, many artifacts are made during the process. These artifacts can be used for completeness for example, or for guide thinking. They can be also used for an audit trail. Artifacts can be different things, from documentation to programs, models, or some other items that a team produced before they started with the implemented system. The meta-model is defined as a ''semantic content of model artifacts.'' If the meta-model is available, it consists of conventions of documents and described graphics used to build the next more advanced models.

If we talk about approaches that are used to develop different systems, we are talking about methods. A method is an activity that includes several stages. These stages are the definition of a system, the way of building the system, and finally- the implementation of the system. The method is better described as a framework for the system. The method has to be logical and it is generally used for the construction of the processes. In this case, we are talking about meta-processes which mean that the framework is actually a process that is used to model another process. Every method has components that can be micro and macro. The macro aspect refers to the overall time frame for work performances and the workflow. Micro components are components that are important for the details such as thumb rules, patterns, and rules for the design. These design rules, for example, help teams to organize and have a set of instructions while developing the system. Some rules describe the goals for the system's design, and instructions on what to avoid. On the other hand, patterns are considered to be solutions that a team can apply to a certain activity during the development phase. These solutions are designed to fit problems that usually occur during some activities in a method. Finally, thumb rules are rules that give the team general tips and hints during the system development process.

The terms such as the artifacts, the method, and the implemented system concept are terms used in processes of industrial control. When we apply these concepts to the system's development field, we can divide them into two categories. Firstly, they can be fully defined or theoretical. And secondly, they can use the comparison already mentioned as a ''black box'' otherwise known as an empirical category. Being able to categorize the system correctly is one of the first most important tasks during the system development process. It's because the whole method structure that will be formed and applied later depends on it, and it is different for both theoretical and empirical categories.

If the model is determined using the first principles, fundamental laws, and energy balances than we can say that a system is theoretical or fully defined.

Contrarily, empirical models are determined by the categorization of processes and their inputs and outputs. Using an empirical approach system gets control techniques that can be used to cause or prevent certain activities in certain amounts. The empirical approach is usually used to construct a model based on outputs and inputs that were provided by experimenting, without laws that define the nature of the system or its properties, and without any recourse. Unlike theoretical, empirical approach doesn't need previous knowledge of the system even though it can be helpful. This is why this kind of system is compared to a black box.

Theoretical approach	Empirical approach
It doesn't rely on experimentation. Experiments are only used if the measurements need to be extended or if the model development specifically implies it.	Contrarily, the empirical approach usually uses less measurement.
The theoretical approach gives us details only for parts of the processes that can be influenced by action control.	It is based on experiments and uses the results of these experiments to determine estimations for models that have unknown parameters.

This approach is based on the promotion of understanding the internal work of the process that has to be fundamental.	Unlike the theoretical modeling, the empirical approach gives us information about the whole internal process during the system development process.
The theoretical approach can't be implied without complete and accurate knowledge about the process, and it is not good for processes that are poorly defined or complicated.	It doesn't treat the process as a fully defined set of predetermined inputs and outputs but like a "black box".
The theoretical approach produces linear models. If a team wants to produce a nonlinear model with this method they have to fulfill special requirements.	Empirical modeling doesn't require complete previous knowledge. It is based on the fact that we can obtain outputs only as a response to the inputs we set or changes that we made to those inputs. It is used in complicated processes that are not fully defined or understood enough, and it produces both nonlinear and linear models without special requirements

This is why it's important to properly categorize the system. If the system has characteristics that fit the empirical approach, the management is distinct and effective in different terms than the theoretical one. When the system is established to be empirical, the team will use a set of measurements and external control that will help them to better understand activities that have loose definitions. The empirical method is designed to have better insights into processes that work unpredictably and change during the development phase.

The theoretical approach was used in the past where methods were described and applied like the whole system is understood and unchangeable. Lack of proper measurements and various problems were a direct consequence of this incorrect approach. Also, if you try to treat this ''black box'' in an empirical approach as a fully defined process, you will get the same result which will end up affecting the productivity and the final product of the system development process.

Starting with a Scrum

Scrum is a framework that uses three artifacts and three ceremonies and has three roles. The artifacts that Scrum uses are sprint backlog, product backlog, and Burn-down chart. Three ceremonies of the Scrum are daily Scrum, sprint planning and sprint review. And the three roles of the Scrum consist of Scrum master, product owner, and the team. The most important thing, in the beginning, is that everyone understands the roles and responsibilities they are assigned to, and what is going to be the overall operational flow of the Scrum.

Sprints represent intervals of work which usually last for 30 days (sometimes less). The alternative name for these sprints is iterations.

The practice has shown that the team is not able to have an effective overall view on the project segments for more than 30 days. During an agile process, the iteration is used to deliver a ''finished'' functioning software. The term ''finished'' is used because even though it isn't the final product, at the end of each iteration that version of the software has to be deliverable to the customers. This also includes tests to prove that the software works. However, the practice has shown that today only half of the Scrum implementers can deliver fully developed and tested software at the end of the iteration. The data from CMMI Level 5 Company showed that if the team fails to create this kind of deliverable by the end of the sprint, the development process will be doubled.

Being able to deliver a version of the product that can be shipped to the potential customers by the end of the sprint has some requirements. The practice showed that these requirements are:

1. The team has to get a completely clear set of priorities from the product owner. It is desirable that there is only one product owner and that he has established priorities that are consistent and fixed for the length of that individual sprint. If the team gets different priorities and changes during the sprint, you have overworked people and this causes delays in decision making. This means that productivity will decrease. Contrarily, the implementation of Scrum and resolving this issue has proven to double the productivity of the team.

2. The product backlog has to be ranked by value. The product owner has to deliver the list and make sure that there are no changes during the sprint. Ranks of the features in the product backlog are determined by their business value.

3. The implementation of these lists provided by the product owner must be estimated by the development team. Even though the experts can estimate the time needed to implement features, they can't estimate the knowledge or technicalities that the original development team has or will use. That is why in Scrum the team determines the time frame for implementation. Factors that can influence the team's estimation are competition, motivation, general relations between the team members, ability to resolve conflict. There are also things like team spirit or losing a staff member due to unpredicted circumstances. All these factors can affect productivity and stability, so they can't be excluded from the estimation.

4. The burn-down chart is a chart used to follow the number of features that can be delivered at the end of the sprint. This chart is used to calculate the overall feature implementation during each sprint individually. Several delivered features for one sprint is called the velocity of the team. The duration of the sprints has to be the same to calculate the velocity. Product release plans are made relying on these results which is important for the product owner. If the sprint length isn't constant, the release date is unpredictable which is bad for both management plans and customers.

5. One of the most crucial factors for successful feature implementation is the ability of the team to work without the involvement of external parties such as management, leaders of the project, etc. Disruption causes chaos and prevents the team from clear and focused work.

Unfortunately, only 10% of teams in the whole world can meet the standards for Scrum implementation. However, any descriptions about Scrum implementation have to be a part of SVP in product development. SVP is connected to IDX System Corporation that has a development team that grew from 600 up to 2000 people. That's where the Scrum was presented immediately to all developers. The consequence was a renewed structure in the organization so the Scrum could be coordinated properly. The Scrum team, in this case, was called the Scrum of Scrums. A management position in the previous organizational structure was replaced and managers were introduced to their new roles as team leaders in Scrum implementation. Furthermore, the engineering directors were placed to be the leaders of Scrum of the Scrums.

During the period between 1996 and 2000, Ken Schwaber was a consultant for different parts during the reorganization and Scrum introduction to all members that participated in the system development process. Units of developers at the time usually had less than 100 people per unit. Managing these group sizes was effective in the Scrum of Scrums. In this case, the product owner was, in fact, the architect and he designed the product backlog. Every unit had its own product owner who created business architecture for the product backlog of that specific unit. If we talk about the SVP level, we have to mention that their team was built from teams of directors and VPs that had periodical meetings. Their purpose was the coordination of activities according to the product owner's product backlog business descriptions for every individual business unit. Having the background enabled the SVP to create a global product backlog for all units.

Iterations were planned to last for one month, for all units. The product owner for each unit was responsible for the deadline being met and that every unit had to give 10% of their resources to the teams that address global product backlog. This enabled units to work under the same conditions and toward the common goal and framework. When it came to software integration for all units, the same virtual strategy was used. This strategy enabled senior developers to work with Scrum teams in all iterations.

Scrum was designed to create a working environment in which a team won't have separated or specialized parts. This approach gives everyone a chance to get in front of line production. In SVP the team was able to provide successful coordination for the Scrum of Scrums and all of its business units. Still, it wasn't the most optimal solution for the global product backlog that all units used during the system development process. Nowadays, there is a more efficient solution and it is reflected in having a Meta-Scrum team above the Scrum of Scrum one.

This Meta-Scrum team is under the direct command of the main (chief) product owner. Meta-Scrum includes companies' stakeholders and incorporates them into their work. Meta-Scrum meetings are organized at the end of every sprint. The purpose of these meetings is to review the results of the sprint and the work of all units and to revise the product release strategy according to these results. Only on Meta-Scrum meetings, can members decide whether they want to change something or to start the new Sprint. They also have the authority to stop the sprints if they conclude that the product is already finished or if it is useless to continue the development. The highest role in the Meta-Scrum team is the Scrum Master who is usually the CEO of the company.

Scrum in terms of outsourced, distributed and linear scalability

The development process of the software can be scaled linearly across geographic properties and team size in development. This was explained in two case studies that were published in 2007. A project that was developed by StatSoft and SirsiDynix had more than a million code lines. This code was further sent across Russia, Canada, and the United States. This project doubled its velocity by doubling its development team. Engineers were brought from Saint Petersburg (Russia) and they increased not only the team size but also the software production and delivery. In the CMMI Level 5 Company, a similar effect was produced. They implemented Scrum in Denmark's Systematic Software Engineering. Their teams were agile, so their productivity was increased only in terms of size and amount of individual work. This means that in CMMI Level 5, the same productivity level was calculated per developer whether they were working in the small team or in a larger one. However, after the Scrum implementation, the costs of the projects were reduced by 50%, and the planning expenses were cheaper by 80%. Employers and users were happier and more satisfied with their work conditions and environment so the company converted their way of work and adjusted it for Scrum implementation in terms of training and documentation.

A combination of CMMI and Scrum to produce suitable and disciplined working environments for the large project was explained in a detailed paper published by Systematic Software Engineering in 2008. This paper described that creating such an environment allows teams to increase the velocity and overall production which was proven on CMMI's smaller teams. Systematic Software Engineering showed the successful implementation of

Scrum that has become institutionalized in a big company such as CMMI Level 5. Even though the consistent model can be achievable in any company, it was proven that it has to be adjusted to the specific company. Scrum acknowledges localized and individual company structure and gives specific inputs for the company's adjustment through inspection and adaptation. It questions the organizational structure in the company's management has to come up with the best structural solution to use Scrum properly and use it as an advantage.

If the company wants to implement Scrum, it is highly recommended not to do it without an experienced trainer of Scrum. Having an experienced Scrum implementer will help on multiple levels and will create the best strategy for a specific company.

When we mentioned agility of the team, we referred to the team's ability to deliver maximum value in terms of business for the shortest amount of time possible. Usually more than half of the original requirements change during the software development process. On the other hand, half of the features incorporated into the final product are actually never used by its customers. That is why is important to have teams that can adapt themselves to the required changes that include avoiding features that are not used and to self-organize accordingly. If these requirements are met the results would include less time to deliver a product, it will increase the quality of the product along with the satisfaction of its users. Also, the developers would feel more relaxed and they would create an enjoyable working environment. The reason for this is that Scrum practices originated from the best Japanese manufacturing development strategies.

Scrum sets a goal of achieving the ''Toyota Effect''. It means that a Scrum team will deliver four times more software codes that will be twelve times better in terms of quality in the time frame of one sprint (thirty days or sometimes less). These results need to be achieved during all sprints needed for the project closure. When implementing the Scrum, the team agrees to have intensive daily meetings that last 15 minutes. In these meetings, people like designers, coders, marketing testers, software analysts, etc meet to discuss. Even the support staff has to attend daily meetings. The purpose is to keep track of everyone's progress and create a consistent connection between all segments of the development team. As we already mentioned, there is a list of the product's backlog items that need to be delivered to the team. In every sprint, the backlog list has to be reprioritized, and then the features that are first on that list are developed in the next sprint.

Features in the product backlog are predefined at the beginning of the sprint. This includes the tasks that are required to implement the features. It also includes an estimation of the time frame needed by the development team that is always multidisciplinary. Not all tasks are defined immediately. Some of them need more time so they are designed in some later stage of the sprint. In this case, the sprint evolves. Still, if the team is skilled enough, they can make an estimation of the timeframe that is more than 80% accurate. The amount of work needed for correct time frame estimation includes techniques that are based on their most recent planning and research resources.

If team members create an environment in which they pull the list of required features to work just on time, that means that a team works in a lean production environment that uses the ''pull'' system. At the beginning of every sprint team member define or pull several features from the product backlog they can deliver by the end of the sprint. The key is to determine an exact number of features that the team can commit to executing and to allow them to choose the tasks. This is a dynamic process and it helps the team to keep a minimal number of tasks possible. This way the work in progress is at its minimum too and integration issues can be avoided in the later stages of the development. Daily meetings during the sprint phase are used to evaluate the challenges and problems of each team member. This results in an increased ability of the team to self-organize and to succeed in delivering the maximum number of features possible in real-time. In Scrum, daily meetings are based on answers to three questions, and every team member needs to provide their response.

The questions are:

1. What did you do yesterday?

2. What will you do today?

3. What blocks, problems or impediments are getting your way?

A coherent and well-connected team will be able to reorganize their plans for the day after a brief conversation based on these questions. Also, this system gives the Scrum Master or the team leader enough information to calculate the Burn-down chart that we'll explain later.

If the team can change the velocity of their work then the Burn-down chart can calculate the delivery date of the product. This means that a team needs to have points of acceleration or deceleration during the sprints. A classic Burn-down chart is made of time needed to complete the tasks for software that can be delivered to potential customers. These tasks are considered to be outstanding and they need to be executed by the time the sprint ends.

Developers divide their tasks into small parts and then enter them into the backlog. This way the Scrum Master keeps track of active daily work and remaining daily work during each sprint. For example, this backlog enters are something similar to entering updates to your Excel spreadsheet every day. Work that remained for each day is gathered and generated into the cumulative backlog. Today, Scrum has developed methods that need only one minute to make an update. Every developer enters two items for their active task data. They must enter the percent of the completed task for that day and the time that remains to finish the task. Entering these two data allows an automated system to create and calculate the Burn-down chart based on the information it gathers. That's how the Scrum Master can see the decreasing number of uncompleted features for the sprint. Additionally, the chart is used in Scrum daily meetings to determine mechanisms for maximizing team production and completion of the so-called cumulative backlog.

Practice showed that in Scrum, project planning is used to produce consistently faster ways to achieve the ideal product. That is why it is considered to be superior in terms of paperwork, efficiency, and effectiveness.

Burn-down chart

Scrum is considered to be the only methodology that is agile and officially formalized to be published as a pattern for the organization in software development systems. A scrum is an approach based on carefully documented mechanisms designed to achieve the best results possible. It is a process that nurtures the assumption of changeable requirements during the development phase. This means that the whole strategy in Scrum is based on the fact that the priorities and specifications WILL change from the moment the project starts until the moment the team delivers the product. Some experts compare Scrum with the Requirement Uncertainty Principle.

This principle says that the requirements for the creation of a completely new system can't be known if we don't have feedback from users. Scrum uses this principle and includes inevitable uncertainties that will occur during system development. These uncertainties are inherent and they are always connected to the products and processes of obtaining those products. On the other hand, we have Wegner's lemma or mathematical proof, which says that an interactive system can't have complete and unchangeable specifications. The Burn-down charts built these days are oriented on objects and their implementation. Environmental variables influence these objects and define their use. This means that object-oriented systems can't be implemented without the direct influence of environmental inputs, which define the final output of the process itself. This can be used to define an interactive system.

Traditional methodologies, for example, assume that the requirements of the system can be defined in advance and that they are unchangeable. These software approaches are based on the premise that users already know what they want and that they don't need to see it before receiving the final product. In traditional methodology observes the development system as an absolutely predictable process that can be fully defined. We can see that these premises are flawed and that they don't correlate with the mathematical proofs or principles that we mentioned before. Results of implementing the traditional approach state that around 31% of projects developed this way were doomed before they reached their final phase. The most commonly used method of the traditional approach was a waterfall.

Scrum, on the other hand, is represented as an approach that evolved during its implementation in the first five companies. The key advantage of Scrum is that it allows you to learn along the way and to build up and use that knowledge and improve your Scrum implementation. It is described as a scalable and already proven methodology that guarantees success. Scrum is designed to support the Uncertainty principle and to make system development agile and lightweight.

The first Scrum was implemented in Easel Corporation in 1993. It was used for software teams where Jeff Sutherland was a VP for object technology. First Scrum was designed as an object-oriented tool for the first time. This tool was also used for analysis, and it was incorporated as a round-trip engineering.

The second Scrum was developed in VMARK. This Scrum now had the automatic mapping of object-relational products and it mapped enterprises in developing environments. Jeff Sutherland had some help in evolving the second Scrum. His assistants were Jeff McKenna- developer and John Scumniotales who was a programming consultant and later he became a development team leader in developing object-oriented tools using Scrum. VMARK bought Easel Corporation in 1995. Scrum was in its second phase until 1996 when Sutherland became a VP of Personal News Page development. Then Ken Schwaber joined his team the Scrum was incorporated into individual development processes. Schwaber was founder of Advanced Development Methodologies at the time.

1996 was also the year when Sutherland brought Scrum into IDX systems. He gained the place of senior VP and was in charge of product development and engineering. In that period, IDX was one of the greatest software companies dedicated to healthcare. It was also the ideal ground for Scrum implementation in multiple teams. That year, around 600 people were developing new products. The product number increased to dozens.

Patient Keeper Company started implementing Scrum in 2000. This company was a big wireless (mobile) platform for healthcare in which Sutherland had become CTO. This was the fifth company where the Scrum was fully and successfully implemented. All these enterprises were different in size and profitability. Scrum was tested in all stages of these companies whether it was a startup, middle-sized firm or large and widely successful corporation. In every case, Scrum helped these enterprises to deliver their products to the target market.

Software Development that is known as "All-at-Once"

The introduction of the Scrum methodology at Easel Corporation was caused by a few key factors. First of all, authors like Peter De Grace and Leslie Hulet reviewed the traditional approach known as Waterfall methodology in their book called ''Wicked problems, righteous solutions''. In this book, the Waterfall approach was described as flawed. They explained that this methodology can't be functional in software development systems today.

First of all, in today's development systems, we don't have fully predetermined requirements. Also users, today don't know if they want the product before they see the first version or rough version of the software that is being developed. As it was already explained, requirements don't stay the same during the whole process, which means that there are chances that the team has to be able to meet. Technology also develops fast and it makes implementation less predictable. That is why strategies have to be flexible.

This book also reviewed "All-at-Once" methodologies in software development. These methodologies were object-oriented and they were fit to resolve problems that might occur in implementation during the software development process. ''All-at-once'' methodology uses the assumption that all requirements created for the software are a result of simultaneous work of analysts, designers, coders and testers that implement all of their created features into one final deliverable system. A good example of the simplest model created with this approach is one supper programmer that can create an application in all its phases-from the beginning until the end. This way, all stages of the process are in one head and all aspects are covered by it. It represents the fastest way to deliver a complete product that is consistent and qualitatively representative.

The next phase in the All-at-once method can be observed as tying two developers with handcuffs. This is also known as pair programming in XP practices. The purpose of this pairing is to have two programmers delivering the whole system. The practice has shown that the programmers delivered better-written code that was more efficient in terms of maintenance, usability, its extensions and flexibility of the system. They performed better results in comparison to larger groups of programmers working together. The real challenge was to get similar results with larger teams in all aspects mentioned above. The goal was to get bigger teams to do it, and then have a team of teams do it. The all-at-once methodology was based on Sashimi, Scrum and Japanese approach for product development. It uses prototyping production while building software and it implements Sashimi to integrate all program pieces into one fully functional system. Also, All-at-once uses iterations to provide higher productivity while developing the software.

All-at-once was somewhat inspired by Hujiro Nonaka and Hirotaka Takeuchi. They described their implementation and management of Scrum through a team-building process. For them, the idea was to build a team that will be self-empowered. The whole team had to build its own global view for the product and develop it daily. This way of team management was successfully implemented in worldwide companies such as Canon, Honda, and Fujitsu. Peter Senge later promoted this kind of approach at MIT, but it already had impacted the way of approaching the systems in general. Furthermore, Peter Wagner from Brown University released a publication, which implies that no interactive system can be fully defined, tested or specified because it responds to external variables or inputs. This publication was previously mentioned as Wagner's lemma or mathematical proof. This lemma is a confirmation that inputs can't be predicted completely and that methods that use entirely defined systems such as Waterfall won't be successful in developing object-oriented software.

Another example of successful Scrum implementation as an object-oriented method can be found in James Coplien's publication. This paper describes the development of Windows' Quattro Pro software. It is said that the team that was working on the development of

Quattro made one million code lines in the C++ program in just 31 months. The team had four members at first, and later the team gathered eight people that were working together until the end of the project. If we divide the number of produced lines of code, we can see that each team member created a thousand deliverable code lines per week. This is considered to be one of the most productive software development projects ever made. This, hyper-productivity of the team was achieved by intense daily meetings and interactions. Meetings were obligatory for all team members including external ones. Quattro Pro had its project management, developers, product managers, documenters and quality assurance members on these daily meetings.

Punctuated Equilibrium effect on Software Evolution

Let's get back to Easel Corporation and its Scrum implementation. As we suggested before, one of the Scrum's main characteristics is it daily meetings that include all team members. In Easel, these meetings were accepted and implemented with discipline, which allowed everyone to become familiar with the Scrum pattern. The effect that appeared as a direct consequence on Easel's working development environment was named the ''punctuated equilibrium'' effect.

This means that a component in the design environment fully integrates, the software will evolve rapidly. This evolution will be highly adaptive and emergent, and we can compare it to the punctuated equilibrium found in some biological species. In terms of biology, punctuated equilibrium means that a change will occur in intervals that are divided with periods of stagnation. In computer science, this effect means that, the system in development requirements change in these intervals, and that punctuated equilibrium means that the change is ongoing and applicable to the whole organism (system).

Direct effects of punctuated equilibrium are not visible immediately. Some subsystems need to evolve. These subsystems start working together and that's where we see the real impact of this phenomenon. The punctuated equilibrium was especially visible in teams who were working in an environment that was based on components. Additionally, these teams used tools that were adequate for business engineering processes. In this case, Scrum merely accentuated the overall effect that the punctuated equilibrium made. When every member of the team sees what others are doing they start to interact and discuss solutions to maximize their productivity and they come up with solutions to provide better and faster results for each other. For example, if one developer sees that his fellow teammates can shorten some part of its code and helps him, it will help not only that one developer, it will accelerate the whole team.

At one point, the punctuated equilibrium accelerated productivity so much that the project managers needed to slow them down. Several Scrum implementations showed the tendency for hyper-production, but Easel Corporation is one of the most dramatic examples.

Software evolution was stimulated with the technique called the Sync steps. To understand what Sync steps are, we have to know the definitions of terms like project domain, package and topic area.

In Scrum, the project domain is defined as a set of different packages that will be used to release the final product. On the other hand, the package was described as functional pieces used by customers. Packages later evolve from work in topic areas, which leads us to their definition. Topic areas are perceived as object components in business, and every change in the system can alter some business component. Refactoring of these components can cause one change that can create a ripple effect on the whole system. This refactoring without causing the ripple effect is known as Sync steps in Scrum.

Chapter 6

Scrum as One of the Original Agile Processes

We can say that Scrum isn't complicated. There are few practices and they are all very straightforward. However, proper implementation of Scrum is hard because management has to follow project reality rather than their plans. As it was already mentioned, Scrum consists of Scrum project description and Management software. This software provides the support that is automated for some of the project activities. So, we can define Scrum as a methodology that has a complete guide for the management of products and their development. One of the Scrum characteristics is its scalability because it can be applied to large and simple projects, and it is useful whether your project is complex or simple.

First of all, Scrum is considered to be an agile process. This means that successful development has a high probability if the Scrum is properly implemented. This probability stays high throughout all stages until the project reaches the point of chaos. When the chaos is achieved, there are no methodologies that are adequate for its management. Through previous chapters, we could see that the Scrum methodology is made of phases and different activities for each phase. To review, there are four phases in Scrum. Those phases are planning, then staging and development, and in the end, the release of the product. When you are planning and staging the project, you are in fact preparing work that needs to be done in the development phase. In this, the third phase, activities need to be fulfilled iteratively. In each Sprint (iteration) team needs to create a product that can be potentially released. It was previously explained that Scrum uses roles and artifacts for its project management. It was also pointed out that Scrum uses them to form groups within phases to define and manage activities on higher levels. All activities are assigned to certain roles.

In Scrum, activities are described but not defined. You will find what to do, but you won't find how to do it since we are talking about agile methodology in the first place. Scrum can provide guidance, but without experience and flexibility of management and the team itself, activities can't be completed. To have successfully finished the project, you need to have an inspection for circumstances that are individual for each project. Be mindful of the fact that Scrum is a guide not a recipe for your project. The most significant aspect of successful implementation of Scrum is having well trained key management roles. It means that you need to have a customer (or Product owner), project manager (in Scrum it is a Scrum master) and in the end the development team or teams if it is a larger project. Training is mandatory because it gives these roles an insight for the intelligent implementation of Scrum methodology to the project.

Agile processes are non-traditional processes that are used to build systems and develop complex products. Group called The Agile Alliance represents a certain number of experts in the industry. These experts were the first to employ these kinds of processes and they basically developed them. The term ''agile'' was introduced at

Salt Lake City Utah meeting in 2001. However, Scrum belongs to one of the original agile processes even though it was used during the early 1990s. After Scrum, many other agile methodologies emerged. Nowadays we have Crystal, Extreme Programming, Future Driven Development, Adaptive Software Development, etc. Thousands of projects today have employed some of these agile principles. Still, Scrum includes all project management activities that are used in any agile process.

In Scrum, management needs to implement distinctive methods that are not used in the traditional approach while developing a product or a system. Every project needs management in terms of planning and initiating the project along with the justification of the project's goal. When it comes to traditional management, these roles have additional responsibilities such as writing reports, finding resources, ensuring that the time reports are made when needed. The traditional manager is the one that assigns tasks and presents deliverables at the end of the project. Contrarily, in Scrum, the project manager (Scrum master) is in charge of Sprints and coaching of the team. It is also responsible for the release management and removal of impediments if needed. If you compare the traditional project manager role with the role of Scrum master, you'll see that in Scrum, many traditional responsibilities are not necessary or they are just irrelevant for Scrum implementation.

Example: Traditional management vs. Scrum

One energy company wanted to initiate a new project. In the following text, we will explain all the activities that were done to start the project. You will be able to recognize some distinctions between agile and traditional project management.

Firstly, the Product Owner (customer) and the Scrum Master (project manager) considered implementing Scrum through formal training. Later they gave up that idea since it was too academic and they thought that the team would have a problem with applying that knowledge to the project. The project manager compared it to the bike drive. He explained that Scrum can tell you how to drive the bike, but you won't be really able to drive it until you experience it yourself. You can't balance and move forward before you sit on that bike and drive it. When it comes to agile processes in general development teams need to get the feel of real experience. If the implementation of Scrum, was just blindly following the description then it wouldn't be that flexible at all. That's why the Scrum master tried another approach. He wanted to implement the feeling of agility. According to him, this way the practice would be easier to remember and they would fit. So he wanted to start the previously mentioned project with a workshop. Traditional project managers weren't very comfortable with that idea; they wanted more time to think things through and more time to discuss. Even though they were opened to try an agile method, for them it wasn't worth a risk since those were their real jobs and project that is important for them and for the company. They couldn't see the positive outcome for this kind of agile approach since they couldn't establish how they'll know if the teams do all that they need to and get the job done.

When they heard about the workshop, traditional project managers were worried. For them, it was inexplicable that there are no project plans or PERT charts. An additional worry for them was the fact that they were not familiar with the project teams since all development team members were new to the company and brought from other contractors. They considered the whole initiation of the project too risky and they couldn't see the positive outcome out of it.

The workshop was organized through 10 segments. The first one was to present an overview of Scrum and XP and introduce the agile concept in general. Then the customer (or the Product Owner) presented its business domain. The Scrum master than explained the concept of the product backlog, what is sprint planning and what is a sprint. During the workshop team members made short introductions and defined product backlog together with the Product owner. Reminder: in previous chapters product backlog is defined as a list of prioritized requirements. In this workshop team members and the Product, the owner made a list long enough to sustain several sprints (sprints are usually limited to last for one month). They all brainstormed about functionality that needs to be built by the second sprint afterward. After the brainstorming team defined their general tasks (they made a sprint backlog) that they have to finish by the end of the first sprint. This means that the team had to turn the backlog they choose into work power. After these segments, the Scrum master presented the concept of daily Scrum, what does end of sprint mean and what are management topics. Scrum master also presented another agile methodology called Extreme Programming and explained how this process can be used together with Scrum. Actually, he used Scrum to wrap engineering practice in Extreme Programming. At the end of the workshop, the development team and all team members started with their first sprint.

Traditional managers have a completely different view after the development team started to define their work for the sprint. They felt relief when they realized that the team itself defines their tasks and the project manager doesn't have to assign them. The definition of the tasks for the sprint started with the review of the backlog. This is where the development team had to give its thoughts about the coding and functionality of the tasks for the work that needs to be done by the end of the first sprint. Scrum master just left the team for few hours to consult and gave them the assignment to figure out the rough design for their tasks and to determine and describe how they will make their work functional and productive. This was an assignment just for developers and no one else could interfere.

The first issue with this kind of approach was the fact that the developers had an attitude that they are on the workshop and that the project manager (Scrum master) will give them the pointers on what to do. They were silent and uncomfortable thinking that it is just training. When the project manager stayed silent and didn't provide any other info except that they need to come up with their own solution team was under pressure. After a while, questions and observations started to emerge. Soon the silence converted into the discussion since developers are usually full of ideas and have their opinions about things. This was the first time that the traditional project managers and developers encountered the system in which they were not told what to do, they were asked what they would do.

During the next few hours, developers were brainstorming. They were plotting, scheming and making plans on building the code for the sprint. Even though there was an uncomfortable silence in the beginning, soon enough people were drawing on the board, writing approaches, making designs and defining other things that will help them achieve functionality for their sprints. While these discussions were progressing, the Scrum master was writing down the tasks that the developers were mentioning. From time to time the product owner had to intervene and give some observations or decide if their idea is suitable for the customer. All this helped the team to focus on defining their work tasks better.

After several hours of intense brainstorming, the Scrum master called a time-out. At the end of this time-out, the development team had prepared their work tasks for the sprint. Of course, some aspects needed to be better defined, also, some estimation times weren't as precise as they could be so new tasks could appear, but all in all, the team was experiencing what kind of work is expected from them in Scrum. They developed the ''feel'' for work that needs to be done for all the sprints that will come.

This kind of approach was shocking for traditional project managers in the company because it was their first time to see self-organization at work. For them, it was unbelievable that the team had figured out what to do and self-organized according to their common conclusions. Traditional project managers have seen for the first time the shift in their role. They weren't the ones who told everyone what to do, in agile processes they are mentors and facilitators. After the workshop project managers understood that their task is to guide and support the development team. The whole system was radically opposite of the system they expected and feared. It was the opposite of their traditional attitude of defining every detail before the beginning of the project and making sure that everyone does their part. Contrarily, in Scrum, responsibilities are reversed because the team has taken them from the traditional project manager.

Agile processes and the Scrum

Even though some people have read or heard about Scrum, or even if they were talking about it until they experience how the Scrum works that knowledge is purely academic.

Keep this in mind in case you want to implement Scrum into some new project. The priority is to give everyone a chance to experience it first-hand. And it should be as soon as possible because you can't observe the development of the system like a manufacturing activity. System development won't turn out into the same system all over again. Development, in this case, represents research and activities where teams of skilled professionals make functional products following the requirements of the market along with fast-changing, thus difficult technology. In this case, Scrum can be labeled as a model of control for empirical processes that uses adaptation and inspection that is both empirical and frequent. This principle is used in all agile processes.

All agile processes can be presented as several practices that are simple and deceptive. This means that, for example, developers have to take a test before they write a code that will be somewhat functional. This can be considered as a requirement for many agile methodologies. Another requirement of agile practices is that a developer has to think through the whole specification and design before he starts to write the code. When the code is written, the developer has to test the code to see if it works. This kind of practice is practical because it cuts the requirements that are too pretentious or to difficult therefore unworkable. It is a kind of coding that is driven by testing every piece of code to see if it is functional.

In comparison, Scrum uses one simple and straightforward practice that we already mentioned. It is called the Daily Scrum. This practice ensures that all developers meet every day to review and discuss the status of the project. As usual, every team member needs to report they work for the day, and the report is made by answering three questions that are the same for every daily scrum. The reason why daily Scrums are one of the most important parts of Scrum implementation is that these meetings ensure that every member of the team accomplishes its peers for the day and to report if there were some issues during the execution of the task. It is a way of creating a deeper bond between the teammates and a way to empower their commitment. Daily Scrums are based on honesty and responsibility of each individual in the process. This kind of relationship helps them cooperate, and to self-organize into a productive community that covers each other's weaknesses.

This practice along with many other practices that are equally effective are all based on a theory called ''Agile process deliver productivity''. This theory is a theory about control and empirical processes that need to be controlled; it is based on exponential gain rather than on multiplication of productivity. It measures productivity with iterative and rapid delivery and not with business functionality that is prioritized. According to the theory, this kind of productivity can be achieved only by making features and components in the architecture of the product by the order they are needed. In this case, productivity is not as valuable as the number of code lines written; it is as valuable as the business value of the deliverable.

The root of every agile process is knowledge gained through experience and experiments. These experimentations are mostly a result of emerging changes in requirements or design during the development process. This way, both customers (product owners) and developer teams can self-organize and create a product that will have iterative and incremental value. The self- organization, and emergence are considered to be the biggest threads of all agile processes and they are a direct consequence of iterations, adaptations and frequent inspections that happen during the whole system development process.

Agile Processes- overview

Martin Fowler explained software development as a set of chaotic activities that are usually explained with the phrase "code and fix". This means that the software has a design that is put together as a result of a large number of short-termed decisions; and that its code is written without any thoughts about its underlying plan. This kind of software creation works well when the system isn't big, but if it starts to grow, it is very difficult to add any other features. Also, it becomes common that the software starts having bugs that are not easy to fix. One typical example of this kind of software is when you have completed the feature but the test phase is too long. This longevity brings disaster to the system's schedules and thus makes debugging impossible.

This style of system development was popular for a very long time. Still, there was always an alternative, and this alternative was called methodology. Methodologies are a way of imposing a disciplined process. This is especially important for software development because the methodology aims to make this development process more efficient and predictable. That is why methodology usually implies a process that has detailed descriptions and emphasizes planning as one of the widely used engineering disciplines.

These methodologies have been used for many decades. They weren't very successful or popular because many people criticized them. The usual critique for these traditional methodologies was that there is too much bureaucracy. According to these critics, there are too many things that everyone needs to follow and in the end, the development process is slowed down by so many rules. Therefore, Jim Highsmith introduced the term for these heavy methodologies and named them monumental methodologies. After some time, a reaction appeared. A new group of methodologies has emerged against monumental ones. At first, they were known as lightweight methodologies, but nowadays they are recognized as agile ones. Many people find agile methodologies more approachable because the bureaucratic part is less complicated and reduced. Also, agile methodologies make a useful compromise between having too many things during the process and not having anything during the development process. Using an agile methodology project has enough things going on to get a reasonable payoff.

The main reason why agile methods gained in popularity is because they brought change from monumental methods. The most obvious distinction is that they use less documentation. Agile methods use a small amount of paperwork for each task individually which is very different from traditional methods. Also, agile methods are more focused on code writing. For them, the most important part of the documentation is the one with the source code. Still, less documentation can represent a consequence from deeper distinctions.

The first one is the fact that all agile methodologies are adaptive and not predictive as traditional methods. As we already know, the traditional approach is based on planning the whole process of software development using every possible detail described in advance. This is useful until the first change appears because monumental methods are designed to resist changes. On the other hand, agile methods are adaptable, so for them, change is good.

They can thrive on systems that change to the point where they will change themselves.

Another thing is that traditional methods are oriented on process rather than people. This is not the case with the agile methodology. The agile method is based on people working towards the solution, working with their nature and making a software development process an activity that the team can enjoy.

Structure in Agile processes

Agile processes are those which render requirements that are emergent into a system that is functional for work. During this rendering, agile methods use adaptive and empirical processes. If you imagine traditional methodology, as an illustration, it would be a predefined process in which each team member completes already assigned tasks sequentially. In this illustration, every task has a detailed explanation of what everyone should too and for how long they need to do it. The picture is linear and has places to mark the tasks that are done one after another until every predetermined activity is completed.

Contrarily, we can draw an agile process with a skeleton and a heart. In this case, the skeleton represents a framework for the whole process. This skeleton is made to support iterations and increment of agile methods in general. The backbone of this skeleton is a sprint. Even though in Scrum sprint usually lasts for 30 days, in other agile processes this sprint can be shorter or longer, but they never last over 60 days. The length of the sprint or iteration needs to be limited to the development team can regularly create a product that is shippable to potential customers. The increment is expected at the end of each sprint because that is how the product owner determines the future of the project and its progress. If increment fits the criteria, the project will continue and the changes won't be dramatic. However, if the increment isn't as good as it should be there can be many adjustments that need to be finished before the beginning of the new Sprint. Keep in mind that all adjustments can be made only after the increment inspection is finished at the end of the Sprint.

This skeleton can be represented with the lower circle that will assign to be the sprint. As the output from each of the project's sprints, we will assign the product that is potentially shippable and its increment. We will then mark an upper circle as daily inspections that happen during every sprint. As we know, during these inspections every member reports its status and progress can be adapted following those daily reports. These cycles are repeated until the project is finished or no longer has funds. The purpose of all agile processes is to prepare the design of the project, analysis of the project, writing code and testing it by the end of one sprint. All this work is performed by the development team that ideally needs to be a small, cross-functional group. These ideal circumstances are not easy to achieve that is why most often groups work on projects that have less than optimal options. Alistair Cockburn introduced a new aspect of agile methods in 2002. In his book named ''Agile Software Development,'' Cockburn measures costs and benefits of optimization of the development team. This measurement is achieved through the impact of the teams that are labeled as less than optimal and their productivity during the project.

Agile methods can't work optimally until the whole organization doesn't adopt practices they recommend, even more, if we multiply this to several teams. Communication between all these teams and their coordination can create an overhead. Agile frameworks operate in a certain way. First of all, and we mentioned this many times- the team must review tasks at the beginning of every sprint. After that, the activities that are selected for the sprint are believed to be suitable for increment and to be converted into a functional shippable product until the sprint ends. When the priorities are set, the team is left alone to work and give its best until the sprint is over. When the sprint is over, the team has to present the increment they chose and to show functionality they have built for this increment.

So, we defined the skeleton of the agile structure. Now, we need to define its heart. The heart of every agile methodology is a well-known sprint. It is a place where the most significant processes in the software development process occur. The heart of the agile method means that the development team has a chance to see and evaluate the capabilities of each other. They also have a chance to get familiar with each other's skills. During the sprint, the team has to follow requirements and get familiar with the technology that needs to be used. This connection helps them to come up with the most effective path to get the job done. It also allows them to self-organize since they can review all problems and surprised every day. Development processes are complex which is why this kind of approach tends to be the most efficient one. The team is left alone to find a way to deal with complexity and to find out what needs to be done. The best way to proceed is their decision, which gives them the possibility to be creative. This is why agile processes tend to be extremely productive.

When it comes to traditional project management, development teams usually receive an already devised plans that they need to follow. In this case, the team doesn't have any control over creative processes because the management has that role. They try to predict what would be the best way for the team to achieve the desired goal in the most effective way and in the shortest time frame. Development teams have little or no influence in these plans and their creativity or opinion is rarely used. Additionally, since traditional approaches management tends to plan everything in advance and has a very specific description of activities that can't support change, the flexibility of the development teams or their ability to self-organize is not an option.

Many projects wanted to implement agile methods because but their teams were stuck in preliminary steps while writing codes for user functionality. These steps were mostly referring to a development environment that wasn't set, or hardware and software implementation that wasn't selected. Teams had issues on how to meet standards for external parts such as DOD or FDA. They also had trouble setting system architecture that had the necessary details. The main problem of this kind of planning and task assignment was that, first of all, customers didn't value it. Even though the team knows it's required to do it, the client just sees it as something that is not important. Another issue is that all preliminary planning is done by groups that are separately engaged. They don't work on the development and they don't have any connection to deliverables or increment and its functionality. The third problem was the fact that delivering valuable functionality has to be delayed since there are many unresolved aspects. This means that competition can take advantage of or catch up with the deliverable that needs to be produced.

Since the goal is to avoid this kind of problem, the agile methodology allows development teams to do all preliminary planning. At the same time, the team builds its functionality. It is important to know that agile methods don't forbid the inclusion of external experts. If the development team determines that they need external experts for their work, they can have it for as many sprints as they need. Still, this preliminary planning has to be done in parallel with functionality development. This functionality has to be presented to the product owner (customer) before the project is initiated which is why agile methodology recommends it in this early stage. When it comes to time frame, most often the first sprints need more time for preliminary work. Later sprints develop functionality for the customer along the way and the process is speeded up. Even though it can be developed along the way, this user functionality that works must be demonstrated at the end of every sprint.

In the book named ''The Pragmatic Programmer'' written by Dave Thomas and Andy Hunt, authors talk about a technique that successfully accomplishes this user functionality in early sprints. They called this technique ''tracer bullets''. According to them, it works like this: a team develops one functioning peace within the total structure of the system in the given development environment. When this is done, that single functionality will work form the interface of any user. It will go through levels that are intermediate and reach even the most persistent data in and out of data stores. And then it will go back. With this, ''tracer bullet'' technique teams can demonstrate that the environment for development and its operational work can refine both team and users and allow the development team to define even more successful goals for their future sprints

Chapter 7

Management in Scrum

When a company wants to have a new product or create a new system, they usually hire someone that can make the process faster and efficient. If they choose to assign that role to someone from their internal system, most often that role is given to the head of the department. Contrarily for the companies that are into the product market, they often assign this job to their product managers. In Scrum, this person is called the Scrum Master. To make the best possible formulation of the project and perform the most effective execution, the Product owner (usually CEO) helps IT and engineering departments in terms of staffing and support. When it comes to Scrum management, the first step is to have a project manager or Scrum master that will closely work with the product owner. The scrum master has the role of coach and he or she forms the teams. During the whole process, Scrum master provides guidance and individual coaching to the team and helps in optimizing the productivity of the development team in general. Collaboration between the Product Owner and Scrum Master is significant for maximizing ROI and for controlling the deliverables at the same time.

When it comes to deliverables, the Product Owner has control on the macro level while the Scrum master uses this to help the development team to self-organize on a micro-level. Just like in earlier Scrum implementations, the Product Owner is the person that needs to develop a plan, or rather a roadmap that everyone else will follow. This plan doesn't need to have all the details just the most important elements. All other details depend on functionality and forecast of goal descriptions and its release. Although this first version of the plan should be followed, it changes throughout the project and most often these changes are made daily.

The role of the Product Owner is also to exert risk reduction and control on an empirical basis and as a response to the reality of the project. This empirical system is based on the premise that the Product owner won't try to fit that reality into his or her initial plan, on the contrary, the Product Owner is supposed to be able to perceive the reality of the project and make decisions according to that perception. Like every project in Scrum, iterations are the main way of running the development process. Increments need to be delivered by the end of each sprint, and the Product owner is responsible for managing the business conditions for the project, technology that needs to be used and results that he or she needs from the development team. This information needs to be provided by the Product Owner in detail and at the end of every iteration. The plans that the Product owner delivers for the sprint represents empirical evidence of what development team has achieved and what needs to be done yet.

Mechanisms of control using frequent inspection and techniques for adaptation are also uncommon for many IT projects. However, Scrum gives tips and detailed information about the empirical management of the project. The fact that it is an agile process enables the management to achieve maximized value for the project that needs to be delivered. This means that project managers become

Scrum masters and their role to predict and assign tasks while writing reports and making forecasts is no longer useful. In Scrum, project managers have a new and different role in coaching and guidance. Management influence has some pressure points that need to be considered. These pressure points are mostly used to measure if there was an increase in productivity in ROI. These measurements don't include aspects such as written code lines or points of functionality. Scrum uses practices that help management to stay on top to observe and measure the effort of the development team and guide them in the right direction. The key role of Scrum master is to make sure that the team will be able to respond to any complex situation and make the most valuable system possible.

Project management in Scrum has to establish what the vision of the project is and to set a time frame and release strategy that will follow that vision. In Scrum, iterations last for thirty days each and at the end of each iteration Product Owner has to receive and rate the results. The product owner sets the alterations and adjustments that need to be done following the rating. This aspect depends also on the business environment so the Product Owner has to determine empirically what will be the next steps for everyone. Since assumptions that the projects are unable to predict are detailed and underlying, Scrum has iterations instead. These iterations represent Scrum's way of managing the working results. It makes the management team be constantly present and to search for ways to make the most valuable result while maximizing the productivity of the development team.

Having a basis in planning, inspection, and empirical responsiveness is not a common practice in all IT projects. Still, during the last decade, this kind of work preparation was well accepted and a wide number of product companies use it. Many tips and details can be found on introducing planning practice in agile processes. This kind of tips can be very useful for traditional companies, and they can be found in Scrum guides in most IT shops.

One of the practices is based on formalizing the role of the ''user'' and renaming it into the Product Owner role. The product owner in this practice has responsibility for the ROI of the project. This practice succeeded to resolve the problem that many projects had. This problem is the involvement of the user in the automation of the projects. One of the tips that are best recommended for the initiation of any project is the workshops. Workshops should be three days long and they should start with building functionality of the team and the product. Through these workshops, every member of the team should be familiarized with the Scrum management, roles that exist in that management and new roles that are assigned to all team members. Scrum is supposed to b used within the business unit. This means that people who will use the final product should be those who have an influence on the project in all its stages. They should run the project and make decisions in terms of backlog definition and progress ratings. With Scrum, these users are given a chance to lay out the project and its requirements.

Scrum influences team proactively. If the management is good enough Scrum can be an intelligent way to get the best possible results while keeping the whole team satisfied. Scrum Master and Product owner don't need written reports so they can study them. They need to be in the place where the work happens and to inspect activities of the project and tasks that are done. Scrum abandoned the rote application of project management, which is why such expectations are nonexistent in agile practices in general.

There are many benefits of Scrum implementation. One of them is that the user (customer), or in Scrum-the Product owner has control over the project development. Another benefit is that the Product Owner is the one who makes requirements and changes during the progress of the project.   Scrum is beneficial because it ensures that prioritized functionalities are the ones that are built first. Scrum is focused on functionalities that are prioritized and it emphasizes only those which Product Owner wants to get. This is significant in terms of time frame, budget, and maintenance of the whole project. Additionally, new working functionalities emerge during every sprint, which allows the Product Owner to decide if he or she wants to release some of the already finished features at the preferred time. This kind of system is beneficial for budget management because the project doesn't need to get funds for more than a sprint (thirty days) in advance. With Scrum implementation financial return from the investment is maximized, and it also allows Scrum to identify things that can be done to increase productivity daily.

Nobody should underestimate the implementation of the Scrum methodology whether it refers to its difficulty or its organizational structure. Many decades and an enormous amount of money was spent on traditional project management and its teaching. Whole institutions were developed with the purpose of training and certifying an individual to become professional project managers. In IT sectors, almost every member has either been employed from this kind of management, or they learned from them. Most of IT employees worked on projects where they were subjected to traditional management. This kind of work is reflected in personal IT practices and expectations. Developers that undergo this kind of project work have a certain attitude about project values and interaction with the users. Furthermore, in this type of management, users work with the IT department in a way that they pass the projects ''over the wall''. Many years will pass until the project failure guilt is entirely deflected from this kind of system.

However, Scrum doesn't use this kind of approach. Contrarily, it is straightforward and simple if you wish to resuscitate a single project for example. And the best thing is that the results are better on so many levels. Developers use the process' agility, and organizational structure gets the success that they aspired to. Implementing Scrum into wide organizations is, however, way much harder. It requires careful evaluation, thoughtful implementation, and planning, and almost as a rule, the whole organizational structure needs to change if the company wishes to stick with the Scrum. All these steps return the company's efforts fast which is also one of the greatest threads of Scrum as an agile management process.

Development that is driven by value

The product owner won't start funding the system development project if he or she doesn't have a vision of value that the project and its product will bring to the overall business and its unit. Project plans are made to calculate the cost of the development process and they are the Product owner's estimation of the price, functionality that he or she wants to achieve with the project, what is the desired quality of the product and what are the implementation days for it. Still, these planning activities are considered to be just mechanisms because usually, the Product Owner has to be present during the whole development process constraining costs, justifying missed implementation dates or ensuring that functionalities build during the development phase are by the plan. During this kind of chaos, the value that the project needs to deliver can be slightly forgotten.

On the other hand, in Scrum, the Product Owner is refocused from this kind of mess to the value that the development system needs to deliver. This value is often expressed with a formula in which value is based on the Product Owner's choice in terms of quality, costs, time frame and overall functionality of the project.

Projects that are driven by value have variables that are determined by the Product Owner during all stages of the system development. These kinds of projects leave the Product Owner to authorize development rates for every sprint and make changes following the progress. Changes usually refer to variables that influence dates for delivery and already delivered values. For example, in the case of deregulation, a project that has already started can change significantly. This means that the Product Owner might want to maximize the value of the project and to increase the cost for its maximization.

When the sprint ends, the functionality of the working system delivered by the team are reviewed with the Product Owner. During the review, the Product owner can decide to change and reprioritize requirements for the next sprint. He or she can ask the team to implement the increment they demonstrated at the end of the sprint, or increase future sprint's cost and request additional work on the backlog of the product. Product Owner can make adjustments and decrease or increase the quality of the project by changing the number of functionalities that the team has to deliver during the further sprints. He or she can also stop funding more sprints because the value that they have received isn't adequate for the number of resources that the Project Owner provided for the project.

Well understood management roles are one of the key aspects of successful implementation of the Scrum methodology. This is one of the most critical points for every project that uses any agile process in general, not just Scrum. Without proper management and its guidance, project teams can be formed without some set of skills that are absolutely necessary for the process. Or the project itself can be set on the wrong premises. Management roles in Scrum exist to prevent dysfunctional organization structure and to increase the value and quality of deliverables that the development team needs to build. These roles outline responsibilities for each team member and assign them with activities that need to be done through the project.

Product functionalities that are potentially shippable and their increment

Many people had questions about Scrum methodology and how it can support software system development that is FDA approved, mission-critical, etc. This doubts referred not only to Scrum but to all agile methods used in software development processes. One of the reasons that these doubts have arisen was the fact that one of the most popular agile methods described software construction as a single-use which meant that only organization that develops it can use it. And this development for any software system is mostly used by the organization's internal IT department, or independent information technology organization contracted by the company.

In Scrum, development teams are required to build a product that has enhanced functionality in every sprint. Enhancements have to be shippable in case the Product Owner decides to release or implement that functionality. To be sure that deliverables have working functionalities that are potentially shippable, the team must test every line of the code and make sure that the code works. This code becomes the basis of the functionality and it has to be documented in the user's manual or Help files.

If product enhancement developed for the sprint has some exact use, the organization has to define requirements that are additional for the product and creates standards and conventions that need to be followed. A good example of this is the fact that every product developed to be used in circumstances that can be critical for life has to be approved by the FDA (the Federal Drug Administration). This refers to all products that are connected to health care and its settings if the product is manufactured or used in the United States of America. FDA needs to have some information to provide their approval. Firstly, they need to check if the product has specific functionality operations and if it is traceable. And every time the product gets an increment, these requirements have to be fulfilled for each enhancement separately and be available for FDA approval if needed. Similar requirements are needed for the products that are modeled mathematically and have performances that are not just shown through statistical measurements. These models have rigors that are considered to be and additional feature for every sprint during their development phase, therefore, their increment also has to be potentially shippable.

If the Product Owner wants to implement enhanced functionality, the next step is to establish Sprint activities for the product release. These iterations need to finish increments that are selected and finalize them into a fully shippable deliverable. If product enhancements are approved by the Product Owner as the ones that fit the desired value, further sprints are shorter. We can use the FDA again as an example. If a project has a product that is FDA approved, every enhancement that is developed further for that same product should have deliverables that will be made by the same standards for approval. If these deliverables haven't been made properly, they need to be adjusted to the point where the FDA can approve them so they can be included in the sprints for the product release.

If a project tends to develop a unique product for non-single use, it means that the system development process can be scalable and it will ensure that the team builds enhancements that work and shape them into potentially shippable deliverables. If the product doesn't already have standards, practices or conventions for these increments, they need to consider developing them as a part of the requirements. Increment standards are usually staged as a priority for any enhancement work and they need to be set in the initial phase of the sprint. That is how they ensure that the increment that is developed is potentially shippable and following the needed regulations. These iterative processes in which agile methods are used to develop increments are also known as ''sashimi''. ''Sashimi'' is defined as a slice of deliverable that contains all the characteristics of the final product of the project. The term ''sashimi'' originated from the word sushi. This metaphor is used because just like one slice of sushi is similar to all other slices, the ''slice'' of the product has all properties of the final product too.

Increment qualities

Quest for achieving the best possible quality is still active through many organizations throughout the world although many useful systems are currently available. These are the systems such as CMM, Six Sigma or Total Quality Management. Scrum is also a methodology that prioritizes quality. As we previously explained, in

Scrum, teams have to deliver potentially shippable product by the end of every sprint. This product has to include artifacts that are needed in the type of system in which the team works. If we take the FDA example, one of these artifacts for their approval is traceability of the product. Quality in this context is actually defined through the potentially shippable product. Furthermore, the quality enhancement in this sense has three aspects that are common for any product in Scrum methodology.

The first aspect is referring to the external quality of the product. It has to be fit to the purpose and to satisfy the intended user while providing easy usability. The second aspect is connected to the internal quality of the product. The product has to be designed well. It also needs to have good structure and to be sustainable. Internal quality is measured with freedom of internal errors and maintainability of the product too. The third aspect is the appropriateness of the system. This means that the product has to implement additional artifacts to provide high quality written code. In terms of examples, these additions can refer to artifacts for FDA approval or other complex systems with established standards.

Cross-functional teams are often needed in Scrum. The main reason is the need for experts that have to create both internal and external quality for increments built by the team. For every sprint requirement is the same- build a functionality that is qualitative enough for potential shipping. This functionality has to meet all the aspects mentioned above and it won't satisfy the sprint if this goal hasn't been achieved. This is why all agile processes, including Scrum, use mechanisms of inspection and adaptation. Those who inspect the value of deliverables need to be well aware of the qualities they need to inspect and what Product Owner's expectations for the sprint are. If the enhancement of the functionality demonstrates good quality and looks good for the user but lacks in internal quality in terms of design, doubled code lines or having bugs, it means that the increment is not potentially shippable, it only looks like that. The reality of this increment is that there is more work to be done before the product can be actually released.

If the team manages to achieve both internal and external quality following conventions, standards, and practices that are set, it means that overall increment requirements are met and the product is potentially shippable. This also means that a big part of the work was done during the sprints in the development phase and that the team successfully built a product that fits the desired quality standards. Sprints for release are not as long as development sprints and the number of these iterations is lesser. The purpose of release sprints is to polish already built and approved functionalities.

Contrarily, if the team unsuccessfully applies conventions, practices, and standards in early sprint stages, they won't achieve the desired internal or external quality. This means that the iteration built during the sprint isn't adequate and it can't be suitable to be shipped to the user. This kind of working functionality needs additional work and significant backlog reprioritization to get the quality that will suffice potential shipment.

As was previously mentioned, it is important that those who inspect aspects of a product's quality know what they inspect. In case the product owner (who is the usual inspector) doesn't know that internal quality is also important and approves the product that only looks good, the problem will emerge since the quality aspects are not proportional. The fact is that in Scrum teams are required to deliver potentially shippable product. However, sometimes there is a lot of additional work that needs to be done before this goal is achieved.

Many factors can influence these aspects. Maybe the team didn't get appropriate engineering practices and that is the reason why one or both of the quality aspects are not adequate. The reason can be undeveloped standards for a certain increment, so they couldn't be used in an environment that was targeted (we can take FDA approval as an example again). Pressure from the management can also be a reason that the team develops functionalities that are more than enough in numbers but less than expected in terms of quality.

Whatever is the case, consequences of quality requirements are visible when the project gets to the release sprints. Product Owner most often wants to release the product immediately after the end of the development phase. Still, if the quality of the product isn't good, it is very difficult to predict how many additional sprints the team would need to make a product that will suffice. This is where Burn-down charts are most useful. They represent the calculation of potential release dates in each situation since the chart is made in parallel with the development phase. In Scrum, the Burn-down chart has a horizontal and vertical axis that represents workload and time frame which are divided into thirty-day iterations.

The burn-down chart enables the Product Owner and Scrum Master to follow the amount of workflow across the time frame and predict the amount of time needed to finish the product. This kind of projection is used to make new release strategies and to reflect potential dilemmas in terms of product's quality and functionality of its increments.

We will also consider the case in which the product functionality is developed with the scheduled quality and an expected time frame. During the preparations, the Product Owner has predicted only one sprint before the official release of the product. If all these conditions are met, everything goes according to the schedule without any surprises and the expected release date is the final one.

Another example is having functionalities of the product developed in the expected time frame but with poor internal quality and artifacts that haven't been developed so releasable status couldn't be approved. In this case, if the Product owner predicted one sprint before the official release his estimation has to change. He can't have the exact estimation since there is an unknown amount of work that's left to be done. The product owner can add three more sprints to its first prediction if the work can be done linearly (this rarely happens). Anyhow, few scenarios can happen during these additional release sprints, since no one can predict how the team will induce quality into already built functionalities.

One of the scenarios can be that the design of these functionalities and their internal structure is not good enough. The reason for this can be double lines of code or other inefficiencies in the structure. It can happen that while the team tries to fix one bug, another bug appears, and when they approach this new bug, another one appears, and so forth. The pressure of a deadline that has already been breached is an additional difficulty for the team, which can influence their struggles while refactoring the code, structure, or just removing the bugs.

Another scenario can be that the quality of already built functionalities is sent to the group that is in charge to test and assure it. These tests help to track the bugs and reporting them to the development team, so they can proceed with their work until everything is fixed. Still, the Product Owner has its expectations. According to the Product Owner, the development team should deliver qualitative functionality while working on other, new functionalities, which means that the team is piled up with bug fixing of the old functionalities and developing new ones.

One of the techniques used to improve quality is the implementation of the engineering practice in which the development team that writes the code, owns that code forever. This is found to be motivational for developers to write more quality codes which are clean, maintainable, easy to understand, and most of all sustainable. The advantage of this technique is that the code writers will give their best because they can either be proud of the code, or it can ruin their confidence. Contrarily, some companies think that releasing developers from responsibility for the written code will help them write new code lines and ease their stress. However, the reality is, if you send already written code to someone else to fix it, there is a possibility that those other people won't understand the code since they are not the original creators.

Management in Scrum knows that if the team owns their code forever, they can't work on any new iteration or develop any new functionality until they fix that poorly made code and make it shippable. This is why the Scrum Master and Product Owner in Scrum don't pressure the development team too much in building even more functionalities during the sprint. The goal is to create qualitative increments. This is how both management and the development team achieve understanding and work more efficiently towards the same goals. This kind of practice represents a strong basis for building both internal and external functionalities. The development team even has the authorization to cut out some functionality if they find it necessary to create increments that are potentially shippable with sufficient quality by the end of the sprint. The key point in surpassing this obstacle is not pressuring the development team too much because there will be certain consequences later. These consequences are usually presented as bugs in codes that can cause dissatisfaction with customers or bad product rating and eventually disappointed developers.

Chapter 8

Scrum Structure
(Paths, Phases, and Activities)

Every Scrum implementation has to follow certain paths and it has to be divided into phases and activities. Phases were already defined as groups of work assignments that have a common purpose. Contrarily, in Scrum, paths are defined as a distinctive way of the structure made for the activities that will occur during each phase. Paths are structured following the characteristics of the project. Activities are the actual work and all the stuff that makes Scrum methodology existent. All activities are assigned to certain roles that are responsible for their completion. For example, the Product owner is responsible for the activity of making and estimating the product backlog. This is an activity that is a part of the planning phase and it was assigned to the person responsible for its execution.

When it comes to the lowest levels of work, activities are usually divided into tasks. Tasks can be pretty much everything, make a sequence diagram for example, or any other detailed piece of work that needs to be done. Still, Scrum doesn't actually include tasks. In Scrum, this kind of work is not predetermined; it is empirically induced by those who are responsible for a certain part of work as that work occurs. We will take a Scrum development team for example. The responsibility of the team is to convert certain product backlog requirements into working functionalities. Tasks, however, are established and assigned by the team to each member by their own terms. Every member has a responsibility and it has to determine tasks on its own to get the work done. These tasks can be modified, completely changed, multiplied or cut out during the process as long as they deliver the required result. We can give another approach for phase definition, and observe phases as groups of similar activities which paths depend on the type and characteristics of the project

Planning

Planning is the first phase in Scrum. Its purpose is to determine the vision of the project, project expectations and ways to fund the project. The vision needs to describe in what ways the product will change and influence the business environment and what are the benefits to the customer. It also needs to explain how the product will be introduced to the market. Sometimes planning needs to have phases too. We can take an example of healthcare software that needs to add equipment for digital imaging such as X-Rays and MRI. The vision for the project was an adaptation of radiology operations in which radiologists can discuss and review the condition of their patients having the same digital image. Additionally, they could mark those images and access them whenever they need it.

Vision has a purpose to determine the common context for the product, thus in which environment decisions will be made. The vision of the project is also a resort used to get the necessary funding. A project proposal must show what the benefits are, and how the funds will be implemented most efficiently. Vision can be demonstrated through models, words, spreadsheets and most often it is not too long. Once the vision is presented to the possible fund sources, they decide if they want to financially support the project. After planning, the highest prioritized work is getting the funds, creating an initial product backlog along with the release plan. After that, in this phase team needs to determine technicalities, architecture in business environments and expectations from the project.

Staging the project

Every project has its own characteristics, some projects are large or require big and numerous teams and others are small but complex, with many teams that work together to build software. Some of these projects need a big amount of work to determine the environment that is satisfactory for product development, while others are immediately ready to go. In the phase called staging, a team assesses different aspects of the project. In this phase, the team also creates additional product backlog needed for further development.

Staging has many sub-phases. Every sub-phase represents one aspect of the project and it is assessed as such. During the staging phase, many different paths can be used in each sub-phase. Activities needed for each of these paths are not an actual projection of work. In fact, activities, in this case, are used to prioritize or add requirements for the product backlog. The actual work is a result of these requirements, and that work is performed during the development phase and by the project team. Staging is important because it helps with building mechanisms for coordination and communication between all Scrum units, or between self-organized teams.

Final sub-phases are significant for project initiation in Staging. These sub-phases get the project started. This means that there are enough staff members in each team and that the team already got together with the Product owner to get project details. In these sub-phases products, the owner gives as much information about the project as possible shearing the vision and everything else that is acquired during the planning phase. Sometimes, this means that the team needs to get out and become familiar with the targeted environment. It is a part of the experience needed for the team if they want to understand the purpose of the desired system and its implementation. If by any chance, team members never worked in Scrum before, it is highly recommended that the Scrum methodology is introduced to the team through concrete training.

Development

All activities connected to the complete process of product development are done in the development phase. This phase is divided into sprints that have the purpose of developing increments of working functionalities for each sprint individually. Sprints consist of sprint planning, daily meetings, and daily reviews. If the projects are complex, then the architecture of the software is significantly complex too which means that there can be more than one team working together on software development.

In this case, sprints are used to build a product backlog that will be coordinated by models and designs that were implemented in the first sprints done by one team. This team distributes further context and information about the product to every other team.

If the development environment is upgraded and that upgrades are needed before all teams can deliver potentially shippable increments, the work is scheduled for the next sprint as highly prioritized work by the common product backlog.

This kind of work functions in parallel with the actual development of required functionality. Although the architecture of the work environment is requested in some of the first sprints, every other sprint in this phase also has to deliver working functionality with a suitable increment.

Release

When it comes to the release vision of the project, its functionality is based on a combination of benefits that are expected from the project along with the overall costs, time frame, and availability.

After every sprint in the development phase, product owner reviews if the desired functionality is achieved and what is the right time to release the product.

After all these inspections and reviews, the Product Owner establishes if the conditions for release are met and the project enters the Release phase.

This phase is made of two different kinds of activities. The first one is the activity that sets additional requirements for the product backlog. These requirements should polish the product and convert it from potentially shippable to an actual releasable product. If the development phase failed to meet any of the requested assignments, the product owner addresses more sprints to fix this point.

Another activity in the release phase refers to one or more sprints that need to be added as a consequence of inadequate increments created during the development sprints.

The release phase can be established only after the development team creates working functionalities that suffice final product backlog requirements.

Chapter 9

Tips for Successful Implementation of Scrum Phases

In this chapter, we will address some of the problems that might occur during the implementation of Scrum phases. For example, how can you find a solution to fund some of the problems that have to be resolved without knowing the concrete result, and how you will present the possibility of allocating the funds to the possible funders when some risks and circumstances can't be predicted, but they are still in control from ROI?

The person responsible for the project planning is the product owner as we already know. In big corporations, this role is often assigned to the head of the department. This can be the director of the manufacturing section, head of inventory control, and so forth.

When it comes to product organizations, the product owner is usually the product manager itself because he is already familiar with both software and the products. There are cases in which the product owner is an IT project manager. Usually, this person is in charge of internal infrastructure in the IT sector. For example, the role of the product owner in Scrum methodology can be assigned to the project manager in charge of consolidating servers in the internal IT sector of a concrete company. The role of the product owner is to nurture the product's vision and communicate that vision to all other team members. The product owner also needs to get the initial funding for the project and to constantly work in collecting the resources. This is achieved by making initial product backlog and initial plans for project release.

Why planning is necessary?

Having a plan is the most effective way to determine that the right vision is shared between those who fund the project and those who work on the project and deliver the desired product. The purpose of the thoughtful and carefully crafted plan is to make a bond between all the people that are involved in the project. This bond helps them to evaluate the overall progress of the project and to make decisions that will maximize production within the vision that is established and the context in which decision has to be made.

Having a plan is important in terms of assertions needed for achieving the projected value of the project while respecting the time frameset. Making a plan means that the project manager projects activities that can influence the value of the project. This includes timetables for finishing the project to deliver this value. This kind of setting becomes the benchmark against which the investors and management evaluate the overall progress of the project.

Basics in Scrum project planning

In Scrum, the planning phase is usually made of one sprint that is shorter than others and lasts for 15 days more or less. All practices used in Scrum for backlog sprints or daily Scrums apply to this planning sprint. Outputs that are defined during the planning sprint are used to prepare project documentation and project prototype. In case that prototype can't be made, the planning phase needs to deliver at least the concept proof which is usually one part of the functionality that works in a predetermined environment. So, the first thing in every project is to determine what kind of system project team will build and what the importance of that system is.

In the traditional approach, project planning is made of complete preparation of all tasks in all stages with exact instructions that every member of the team has to do and for how long. Traditional project planning means that the whole development process is predicted thus predetermined. This kind of planning requires scheduled and staffed tasks and activities and the plan itself represents a way to control the project and manage it accordingly. This way project manager has a role to assign tasks to each member of the team and give them work that is planned in advance. Scrum methodology, on the contrary, relies on agility and promotes emergence and self- organization. This way the team can build a complex system even though the business environment can be complicated. Regardless of the initial project requests, Scrum helps developing teams to work with new and also complex, sometimes even untested technologies.

Even if the vision of the system in the planning phase has one set up, the reality of the product and its working functionality will be known after all the activities have started. That is why technology and requirements often change during the project development phase. When there is a new business opportunity, the Product owner prioritizing of the product backlog and functionalities of the final product change. When the Product Owner sees this new working functionality, he or she will decide how that functionality should be released or adjusted. Changes can also occur if the new technology appears in the meantime, or if the one that is already used isn't suitable for the project.

In Scrum, system functionalities are defined only on the highest level. Scrum focuses on functionalities that are first and they are the only ones detailed enough for any kind of proper estimation. Functionality that is defined represents the priority to the development team because that is the potentially shippable product they need to deliver by the end of the sprint. It is also the most valuable one for the business. These functionality details are usually given for one feature at the time. Still, sometimes there can be up to six functionalities that are prioritized in the product backlog.

We already mentioned that in Scrum, management doesn't have any influence on the definition and division of the tasks for the development phase. That is the job for development teams. They need to brainstorm and set the working schedule for themselves, which motivates them and gives them the chance to self-organize. The team can manage itself through the whole development phase and the project manager (Scrum master) is there only to guide them if something is not right. Nobody gives the team a project plan with working details and schedules; they just get the list of functionalities that need to be delivered. The workflow and assignments are determined by developing a team without external influences.

Scrum and new, unfunded or already funded projects

If you start with a brand new project, you will need funding. Every investor wants to know if they will have a return on investment (or ROI for short) and how will they benefit from the project. After they are familiar with these few points, investors will make an evaluation in which they will compare the offered project to all available competing projects and their funding. For better evaluation, investors need to have enough information about the project's vision; risks that project will face and underlying assumptions about the product.

Planning a new project is a way of laying out a vision to the investors against which they can assess their vision of the investment and adjust it if they find it acceptable. It is a set of understandings that need to be common and from which collaboration and adaptation can emerge. This kind of understanding grows into the determination of expectations and measures that can be reported and reviewed.

Sometimes the project can be approved for funding but it still has to get underway. Also, some projects tried to get underway but they were too complex or its technology was stopping any kind of progress.

Some projects have already been approved and funded, but have yet to get underway. Or, perhaps a project has tried to get underway but the complexity of the technology or requirements have precluded any progress. If that is the case, your project representative should be familiar with both users and customers. In the Scrum method, this person would be your Product Owner. You'd give them the authorization to make the first requirements with high priority for the product backlog. After you have found a suitable product owner the next role you need to fill in the role of the Scrum Master. When this person is found you need to start with daily Scrums.

The first product backlog that you need make for your project needs to have basic business functionalities and requirements for technology that you will use. Once you define the technology, the team builds a preliminary design and framework in which the system will operate. When this is over, the team needs to implement determined user functionalities into the framework. Sometimes the team will need to connect the existing database to some functionalities or to make a preliminary database for the project. If these are the circumstances for your project, then the goal of your first sprint is defined. You need to try and deliver the key piece of user functionality using the technology that you selected.

Once when the sprint backlog is in harmony with the project goals, you can create an environment that development needs. This is the time when you set up the whole development team, define the code that will be used and discuss management and practices that will be implemented during the project. In this stage, you also need to start implementing the targeted technology and build a functionality that can be tested on the platform previously made by the team. All these activities are more or less everything that happens during the full first sprint. There are two purposes of this initial sprint. First of all, there has to be a development environment for the team so they can build the best possible functionality. And second, working part of the system built by the development team is actually the deliverable that will be demonstrated to your customers and to the Product owner within the first development sprint.

If you deliver your first working functionality fast and successfully, you will convince both the Product owner and the customers that your project is real. You will show them your determination and real and measurable results and they will get involved. The first sprint is the most important step for every new project because it connects you and your team with the customers and product owners. It introduces them to regular sprint rhythm in which they can always expect deliverables they asked for through their requirements.

The product owner updates the product backlog while the team works on its first Sprint. Keep in mind that Scrum doesn't insist on having a complete product backlog. It only needs to have enough requirements for the duration of several following sprints. Once the customers and the Product owner get the feel from the Scrum approach, they start using longer views of the backlog. If the current vision of the project doesn't follow the reality of the project anymore, the Product owner will make a new vision along with the customers. When they forge a new vision, their product backlog requirements will change too.

In some cases, Scrum is used to get a generated code for an already existing project. In other cases, Scrum is implemented to help a project that already exists in terms of productivity and focus. This often happens because during the development phase teams have issues with building the complex system while following the changes in technology and requirements. It can happen that the team was stuck with trying to deliver documents or models rather than the working functionality for the business. This doesn't mean that the team doesn't have a good development environment or selected technology, it only means that the priorities haven't been properly communicated.

If this is the case for your new project, you also need to appoint a Product owner that represents users and customers. Just like in the first case scenario, this person needs to come up with reprioritized requirements. The next step is also the same since you need to have a Scrum master and to start daily Scrums as soon as possible. The difference is that now you already have the development team and some deliverables. You need to use daily Scrums to find out what are the impediments. Don't be surprised if daily Scrum meetings last for hours in this phase.

The development team needs to talk about all issues and try to determine why they couldn't build the software. You can motivate the team using a simple challenge. Ask them what they can build in a month. This can be a good way to make the team work together and to prove that they can develop the software envisioned in the project. You need to get the team to focus on building functionalities since they are important to the Product Owner. The reality is that the Product owner, in this case, will be impressed by the fact that the team built anything functional in such a short amount of time. The reason for this is the fact that the previous approach team was working for months without delivering any working functionality. This kind of unproductive team can cause the customers and Product owners to give up. The most important goal, in the beginning, is to increase the team's self-confidence and to regain the confidence that customers and Product owners had in the team. This means that this kind of scenario implies that the goal of the first sprint is again to demonstrate any kind of working functionality made with technology targeted on that sprint.

Daily Scrums are used to establish all potential impediments that can influence a team's progress and find a way to remove them. If the team ends up building a working functionality by the end of the first sprint, the Product Owner will decide the requirements for the next sprint meeting and sprint review in collaboration with the team. In practice, there weren't any examples in which development teams failed to meet this kind of challenge.

The traditional approach was based on the premise that a fixed date for product release and a fixed price of the project development are something that can't change. This is why in traditional methods project managers tend to fully define complex systems in all their phases. They estimate those complex requirements can be met with predetermined and contracted activities for each team member.

According to this methodology, if the technology is more complicated than expected, the provider has to ''eat'' that overrun. Also, if the customer changes its mind and asks for different requirements, the customer needs to pay for that change because that is considered to be additional funding and additional control mechanism. This way both providers and customers try to find the balance so if something goes wrong the project won't be out of control.

However, agile processes are based on the uncertainty principle. This means that this methodology accepts that there can't be accurate predictions in complex projects. When the project starts customers and providers are expected to learn together through the whole process. The goal isn't the product, but the business value of that product. Agile practices are open to accepting that some of the initial working functionalities can be irrelevant for the final business value of the product. Sometimes the customers just won't use that feature, regardless of the cost of its development. The fact is that even unused functionality need maintenance which sustains its unnecessary cost.

There are still many customers that construct their proposal requests and evaluations following the concept of a fixed date and fixed price. They use this principle for their contracts too. Companies that have experience with agile practices have to respond to these cases and try to provide the right context and information for the customers. They also need to make sure that there is enough space for the customer to learn more about agile advantages and use them if inclined. Regardless, agile practices always tend to make more productive projects that add more business value to the overall cost for the customer.

We can conclude that the main difference between planning a completely new project and planning a project based on a fixed price/fixed date concept is the level of analysis for the entire system. This also refers to the specifications that need to be made before the beginning of the project. Every bidder has to fully understand some of the basic aspects of the project regardless of its development strategy. These aspects are mostly technical and they refer to business architecture, deliverables of the system and entities that will be employed on these architectures. Every member involved in the project should have a full understanding of the methods, interactions, interfaces and sequences that will be used in the project.

Chapter 10

Purpose, Assumptions, Risks, and Descriptions of Main Activities During the First Scrum Phase

This chapter will address all main activities in the first and most important phase in the Scrum approach. Every activity will have detailed information about its purpose, possible risks, following assumptions and adequate description.

Activity 1: The project

The person responsible: Product owner

Purpose: The purpose of the project is to describe the system that will be developed. This anticipation has to provide enough information for potential investors to understand. It has to be justified well communicated. The project description needs to lay out the vision of the system or the product. It needs to be pointed out that the development will be done empirically and that increments of functionality will be delivered in iterations. Keep in mind that in this activity it is more important to have defined vision of the project rather than having established requirements. During this activity, you need to set goals for the first sprint and for release along with functional and nonfunctional activities for the future.

Assumptions: The project needs a person who is skilled enough to clearly present the vision of the project and its purpose. This person has to be able to get funds for the project and most often this individual eventually becomes the Product owner.

Risks: You shouldn't use too many details in your project specifications. Keep in mind that requirements will change and grow following the business needs. This means that the stakeholders along with the Product owner will have different needs that the development team will have to meet during the process. There has to be enough room for the development team to learn the best way to change the business environment, satisfy requirements set by the management and to keep up with the targeted technologies.

Description: This is the initial activity in any project whether you use an agile approach or not. Still, in Scrum practices, first, you need to define your project. Vision is mentioned many times and not in vain. Vision is used to form the first impression on potential investors and on those who are supposed to participate in the project. Project definition is used as a reliable point that gives focus and context for project teams and guides them through decision making. This is especially significant for some of the following activities in the first phase such as the design of the product and its functionality. Scrum allows the emergence of details which is why project definition is used to provide context and concept rather than already proved hypothesis. Project definition has to be suggestive and to provide guidance while considering possible problems and risks.

The project can be defined in many forms. One of the most frequently used ways to establish project definition is to set it through several aspects. The first one is vision. The project owner has to be able to answer questions such as what the team is trying to do with this project. Or what will that system or product look like and why is it significant. One of the questions that define the vision is to be able to determine what makes that vision valuable or unique.

The second aspect of the project definition is through business operations. In what ways will the project improve the business and will it affect the competition? What is the bottom line of the influence of this project on an investor's business environment?

Another aspect that helps this definition is a product release plan. The product owner has to identify what kind of work will support the implementation plan and what are its key functionalities. This aspect needs to include changes that will positively affect business and what kind of management process will be used to successfully execute these changes.

Defining the project often means that business architecture and its functionality has to be defined too. It is necessary to determine what will be an overall flow of this project for the business and to what degree stakeholders can see the impact of the changes that the project will cause while following approved project vision.

With targeted technical architecture we define what kind of architecture will be used in terms of technology and its functionality. In this aspect, technological stability and reliability are defined whether the team will use it individually or as a part of the more complex system. The following aspect is related to the definition of infrastructure for development, which means that the team needs to know what kind of platform will be used for the development of the system together with its stability.

When it comes to the presentation of the project to potential investors, one of the most important parts of the project definition is to be able to explain ROI (return on investment). You need to be able to point out the benefits that will be acquired as a result of the project and what measures will be available to access these benefits when the project is successfully implemented. You need to calculate the total cost of the project and prepare mechanisms for fund allocation.

Project definition depends on development, which is why even during this initial activity you need to have information such as who will work on the development and how they plan to develop the product. You also need to think about team arrangements, engineers that you can recruit and how can you guarantee that the product will be sustainable, maintainable or enhanced. Keep in mind that you should prepare a list of possible risks and assumptions for every possible outcome.

In order to have a properly defined project in Scrum practice, you need to provide general plans for at least two years of the project. The first year should include descriptions for activities that will be executed and contain milestones for the future backlog. Budget is an important part of this and it should include all expenses and summarize quarters while recognizing possible risks for each quarter. Planning the second year of the project is the same; the only difference is that your risk assumptions and summarization should be made for half a year, not a quarter.

Some additional questions that can help project definition are connected to production improvement, user satisfaction and increase of the repeated number of sales. The definition can also include market influence and its improvement, possible price reduction and all other possible measurement results.

Activity 2: The architecture

The person responsible: Product owner and the team

<u>Purpose:</u> Architecture is used to establish business and technical aspects of the intended system. The team usually uses tools to draw or make models and present their vision of the system they want to develop. Implementation planning, for example, requires business architecture. Contrarily, the system architecture is used to coordinate multiple teams during the development phase. Both of these architectures have enough details that can be used for project management and decision making. Architectural diagrams, on the other hand, are used to demonstrate those parts of the system that are developed during each individual sprint. These diagrams are mostly used in project reporting.

<u>Assumptions:</u> This activity is based on the assumption that both technical and business staff needs to have enough domain knowledge to be able to collaborate with the Product Owner. This collaboration is significant because both sides participate in creating a system architecture that follows the vision of the project.

<u>Risks:</u> Unlike previous activity, project architecture is often too developed and has too many details. A direct consequence of an excessive number of details is overwork in the planning phase. Another shortcoming can be viewed as a restrictive emergency during the further progress of the project. This is why is

recommended that the team provides necessary architectural details during the sprints as they emerge in the system development.

Description: Architecture represents the flow of the system, its interactions, and components whether we talk about technical or business terms. Teams use models to show a better description which is useful for better understanding and decision making. Models made to present the system architecture can't be used to decompose the system later and make detailed code lines because Scrum doesn't use that kind of decomposition.

This activity uses two kinds of models- business and system ones. Both models are made to ensure that the envisioned system is implemented in the best operational way. These models are also used to track progress and to highlight parts that are partially or completely finished by the end of every sprint. It is a kind of visual ROI report.

Activity 3: Design

The person responsible: product owner, team

Purpose: Design is used to expand architectural details so the Product owner can make an estimation of the product cost. The design needs to be completed by classes, sequences, methods, entities, interactions, and development in subsystems. It provides enough information for the construction of the system and what kind of costs that construction will require.

Assumptions: Project can't acquire funding if the product owner doesn't make the initial cost estimation. This estimation must rely on the assumption that there will be potential changes but that the mechanism of change control is collaborated to balance costs and target dates.

Risks: When it comes to risks, cost efforts exceed occurrences that might happen during sprints. Costs have to be determined regardless of the changes in the design of deliverables during each sprint. This kind of development can only benefit directly from increments and sprint since the collaboration and emergence costs are minimized.

Description: Design is an activity in which architectural models are decomposed into detailed artifacts. These previously constructed models now represent divisional requirements for effective cost estimation and efficient cost implementation during the system development process.

Activity 4: Building the product backlog

The person responsible: Product owner

Purpose: This activity aims to make an initial list of requirements needed for system development. The simplest example is making a request that the functionality developed for the sprint check balance before it disburses cash. On the other hand, non-functionality would be the system's response in a sub-second time when many thousand users start using that functionality simultaneously. The environmental response is to multiply the numbers of distributed teams following the shared team environment.

Assumptions: The basic assumption of this activity is that the items created for the product backlog derive from the project vision. These items are later listed according to their priority and developed using that rank. The highest prioritized items on the list have the most details while those that are not important to that particular sprint are vaguely explained.

Risks: Certain risks are inevitable during this activity. The fact that the first few requirements from the backlog are the ones that are developed and expected to deliver can't guarantee predicted value. Actually, during the initial development sprints, these requests are usually delivered just to demonstrate the probability of project realization and to prove that the system can be built. Items that weren't on the top of the list are listed as a coarse grain while the important one is mostly described as fine grain.

Description: The product backlog represents a list of all capabilities, features, functions, and technology of the product that will be developed in the future. This list mustn't be mixed with the task list. Product backlog lists requests for certain functionalities that have to be successfully implemented into the system. That list consists of everything that the Scrum management can think of about the product. List always changes, some items disappear, others appear and it all depends on the progress of the product and the business environment in general. Although there are numerous requests in the product backlog, it is prioritized. Most often these prioritized items have bigger ROI potential while lower items don't.

However, this doesn't have to be always true because it can occur that a lower item suddenly becomes very important thus highly prioritized. These changes represent co-dependence between requirements and they reflect the impact that the users have on development. There aren't insignificant requests for the product backlog. Still, some items stay low on this list for a long time and they may not be implemented at all by the end of the project development process. The product backlog has three kinds of requirements. The first one is the functionality of the product. This means that the Product owner needs one function as the proof of the system performance that can deliver anticipated value following the vision of the project.

Another kind refers to nonfunctional requirements. These are items in which the Product owner requests a demonstration of the product that will have the necessary value. This value has to satisfy operational aspects and to suffice predicted reliability and stability within predicted cost estimation. Environmental items are prioritized to show the capabilities of the product to be successfully developed and delivered. For example, if the development team has never before developed an object-oriented system, that team needs to have proper training, to get to know better the environment and tools that can be used and to learn how to anticipate occurrences during the development phase.

During this activity Scrum management together with the Product owner revise the first established vision of the project. The product backlog needs to gather all stakeholders and let them brainstorm about their expectations of the project. All of these expectations have to be written and detailed. As soon as there are some new details available, they should be added to that item. This way every member of the team can easily see what its further directions are. The product backlog list needs to be managed until there is a good description for every request that is on the top of the list. Since this activity doesn't analyze the system in any manner the item list has a skeletal structure. The real analysis is done in sprints in the later phases of the project. The product backlog is actually a way to establish what the system really looks like. And the development team has a job to figure out how this ''real look'' exactly operates.

One of the tips for prioritization of backlog requests is to always make sure that all nonfunctional items are on the top. In Scrum's first phase this means that the first functionality is developed to be operational but it doesn't to be functional in the system. This makes it easier for everyone to demonstrate that the team can actually develop the presented system. Reprioritizing product backlog ensures that environmental items also have a high priority because the team needs to have a proper environment in which they can create and test the product and its features.

Activity 5: Estimation of the product backlog

The person responsible: Product owner and the team

Purpose: Estimation needs to give an idea about the effort needed for the project development and the number of resources that the process will use. If the estimation is truthful enough it will need every backlog item to be explained in as many details as possible. It is recommended of course that estimation has to focus on highly prioritized items on the product backlog list.

Assumption: This activity assumes that the team and all people with similar skills for product development can be of assistance to the Product owner in its estimation. This estimation emerges as a result of the dialog between the Product Owner and the development team. During these conversations, the Product owner gives all available details about the top requests from the list. These details are later related to every backlog request mentioned and estimated in conversation.

Risks: Estimations need big amounts of time. So there is a risk in spending too much time estimating and forgetting that the goal is to have a general understanding of the total cost of the product rather than individual ones. This way the Product owner will determine if the project is economically appropriate to develop.

Description: Estimation of the product backlog is one of the Product Owner responsibilities. However, he or she can't do it individually. Estimation is determined through collaborative work of development time on one side and Product owner on the other. These estimations include the amount of time needed to deliver working functionality, effort that the team needs to put into successfully completing that delivery and all resource that was used to develop, design, analyze, test and document requested functionality. Estimations are often expressed in days. If you want to make a good estimation you should use your project team. If the team isn't defined yet, a good alternative is external, equally skilled people that can give their estimation. If estimations are made by independent experts that don't have any connection to the project, there is a big chance that estimation will be wrong and mostly irrelevant to those who really work on the project. When the product backlog's priority items decrease, accuracy in estimation decreases too. Estimations are usually good for all highly prioritized requirements since they provide more details. Contrarily, lower items change more often and the time of their successful implementation can't be really given.

These changes in item priorities usually happen when the sprint is over or when business condition change. Customers and users follow and often change their desires so even technology might shift. This is why the best-recommended practice is to spend less time on lowly ranked items and focus on work that needs to be demonstrated at the end of the sprint. In Scrum estimations for the whole project are impossible. Instead, Scrum divides estimation according to sprints just like everything else. This also happens because estimation can be influenced by any new information about the product.

There are many unknowns in Scrum so sometimes reliable estimation isn't enough for the work. Still, if the item is kept as highly prioritized the work continues and the deadline for that functionality becomes the end of the sprint. If the estimated time for developing one requested item is too long, then that item should be divided into shorter backlog items. Estimates in Scrum are mostly used to reflect the level of understanding and thinking about functionalities and their implementation within the originally targeted technology. Usual estimations for higher-ranked backlog items are around ten days while lower items are estimated to be implemented within forty days.

Activity 6: How to adjust backlog estimations

The person responsible: Product owner and the team

<u>Purpose:</u> The purpose of this activity is to adjust product backlog estimations. These adjustments can be viewed as a reflection of factors that can increase the team's effectiveness. In Scrum, the

optimal work environment is assumed. Estimation adjustment forces those involved in the project to understand that there are costs even for suboptimal products.

Assumptions: Adjustment isn't mechanical activity and it doesn't just plug in the factors. Contrarily, this activity is necessary for project management cost awareness. This way, all decisions about the working environment for the team directly impact their productivity and increases the cost of attendance. When the management is aware of this, for them this kind of increase is just a reminder. But if the management somehow hasn't been familiar with this kind of cost the activity immediately provides something called monetary cost for the sub-optimal environment.

Risks: This activity shouldn't be used for quibbling about factors and their values. These values are mostly general and they don't predict individual situations.

Description: Complexity factor is one of the things that are used to adjust the estimated time for any backlog item. This complexity factor refers to the level of that complexity that can affect estimations. For example, there was a product owner who doubled all estimated times that its development team gave him because the whole team was new and nobody was familiar with neither the company nor other team members before the project.

Guidelines for estimation adjustment are just guidelines without scientific tautologies that have to be followed blindly. These adjustments are only used to help make better predictions considering additional variables such as complexity. Two factors can make backlog requirements more complicated. The first one refers to the number of details available for the requirement. The other is the level of agreement between implementation and design for the item and how hard its technology is.

Some product owners think that these factors should be taken into account for initial estimations of requirements. Still, even if you decide to have it, it should be kept separately. Complexity factors can be considered appropriate or general. The general complexity factor can be applied to all product backlog requests and it can be calculated.

If the backlog horizon of the product is known, the complexity factor can be applied.

Generally speaking, that is possible only if the working environment for the team changes but then again, the complexity factor is useless if it is applied to late. This impact should be diminished because the team should master business and technical domains instead.

There are three more complex factors that can be added to the product backlog items. These factors reflect the team's velocity, their working environment adequacy and overhead for their multiple team projects.

To point out, guidelines are given so that these adjustments can be observed as a reflection of the complexity and not be exactly followed. This guidance is useful if the Product owner didn't consider negative influences on development team productivity.

The first additional complex factor is the team's velocity. Let's take an example where the project manager estimates that his development team needs eight days to convert backlog requests into potentially shippable functionality. The project manager's estimation didn't include the fact that team members have never met or worked together. The direct consequence was the team that is unfamiliar with teammates, targeted technology thus unfamiliar with the business domain in general. This severely influenced the team's velocity or productivity if preferred.

When it comes to the working environment adequacy, Scrum has its best effects when the whole team works in big and open space with an appropriate number of conference rooms. On the other hand, if this type of comfort isn't available, the productivity of the team can decrease which means that they will need more time to deliver requested working functionality.

Having multiple teams is the last kind of adjustment that the management in Scrum can resort to. This adjustment is based on overhead communication and management which is caused by many different teams that are working on the development of the same complex project. Even though one group can be very effective, if other teams don't have the same rhythm, overall productivity can't be maximized.

All of these complex factors can be used to sum the total impact on real-time estimation. They can be added together on the same base and multiplied by the team's raw efforts. This way Project owner can get an overall estimate for release strategy.

Activity 7: Release strategy

The person responsible: Product owner

Purpose: is to establish benefits that resulted from developing some of the intended functionalities during the system development process. These functionalities are implemented with the intent to provide increments to both customers and users. Increments are supposed to surpass all implementation costs.

Assumptions: Users and customers have to be able to logically absorb functionalities delivered in the system development and distributed following the appropriate release strategy.

Risks: The release of the product has its price in money and in the effort. This price is paid not only by the development team but also by users and customers who have to learn how to use the product first. Before the product enters the release phase, the product owner has to make sure that the benefits of the release are bigger than offset costs.

Description: The product owner has a responsibility to identify which functionalities will be adequate to make a good construct for the system release. These functionalities if combined properly to make meaningful and usable set are considered to be good enough to be released. If the business tends to change released product is expected to influence positively this new business reality and secure measurable benefits and concrete results. A good product can improve revenues or reduce prices, and these are just some of the simplest examples for the product's potential impact on the business environment. This is why the release strategy has specific assumptions. If the project tends to provide benefits or improvements in the business environment these conditions have to be fulfilled before the product can be officially released.

Still, the Product owner can group product releases into more than one release. Dates of releases are calculated by dividing costs of effort made daily into the total amount of days needed to develop, test, and deliver a working functionality that can be released. Release benefits and estimation can also be calculated if we divide adjusted development and implementation effort for certain functionality with available effort presented with the number of developers working on the project and then add productive hours that those developers need for each day.

With this information Product owner can adjust available effort or requested functionality and establish what kind of release will be done and in which time frame desired functionality can be delivered. The goal is to have a date that will suffice the investor's return on investment in the first place, and then presenting a product that has the value that is expected.

The release strategy in the first phase of the Scrum is usually just an estimation that changes along with the actual sprints. When the real work is done, the release strategy adapts to real team productivity and real value of potential deliverables.

Activity 8: Bid preparation

The person responsible: Product owner

<u>Purpose:</u> Every bid needs to have spreadsheets prepared. These spreadsheets layout all benefits and costs that a project can have. All previous definitions, visions, planning, design, different architecture and estimations are now converted into explicit thus financial content. The bid needs to provide project expectations expressed in numbers. It has to present analytics and quantified assumptions.

Assumptions: It is assumed that the product owner has already made market analysis and that he has valid data about customer operations and their desired quantified benefits. Therefore, the Product owner is aware of all costs that the development of the project will require, including staff costs and general costs for technology or other ongoing section. It is further assumed that the Product owner can express sustainability, maintenance, and enhancement in numbers and calculate them as product development costs.

Risks: Bid will be proportionally successful to the Product owner's competence and his or her expertise in preparing this kind of activity.

Description: Bids are differently prepared for both internal development projects of one organization and product that is developed for commercial uses. In this activity, we will take an example of a product that should be developed for commercial uses and the spreadsheets required for adequate bid preparation. The same principle can be used to internal systems too, with slight adjustments in terms and overall costs.

There are three kinds of spreadsheets included in the bid that has to be prepared for the development of the products that are developed for commercial uses. The first spreadsheet is the projection of revenues and expenses for the development phase, deployment of the product, enjoyment of the product and costs of a system that needs to operate through the customer base. If, however, your bid is for internal organization, this first spreadsheet should just have projections for benefits and costs rather than for revenues and expenses.

The second spreadsheet presents a list of quantifications and assumptions for various underlying benefits and costs of product development. The third spreadsheet should have an analysis of alternative scenarios in terms of the costs and benefits needed for the project development and product release. Every scenario in this analysis should have at least one assumption and solution for implementing the system and successfully delivering the product under those specified circumstances.

Mary and Tom Poppendieck - in their book ''Lean Software development: An Agile Toolkit'' - give many examples in the form of already used spreadsheets that can be beneficial for those who don't have experience in bid making.

How to prepare a fixed price/fixed date bid:

<u>Purpose:</u> Some bids have to include fixed dates and fixed costs for product delivery. This kind of bids also requires a full and detailed list of different functionalities that will be delivered and architecture that will be implemented for the delivery. These bids additionally request extensive spreadsheets that include all underlying assumptions. All functionalities and all costs have to be specified accordingly. Additionally, all artifacts have to be quantified, assessed and already measured.

<u>Assumptions:</u> Different mechanisms can be used to prepare this type of bid. Some can be traditional but also applicable in agile practices thus in Scrum. Even though the bids can include PERT charts, Scrum allows assessments of the workload through functional and nonfunctional product backlog items.

113

<u>Risks:</u> Just like any other method, Scrum can meet all requirements for the preparation of a fixed price/fixed bid. Still, Scrum practices don't have mechanisms that are used for change control which means that they don't modify customer's expectations (known as Scope Creep). This kind of risk is important in Scrum implementation because Scrum works on the premise that the increments are delivered following interaction and customer feedback that is live and functional.

<u>Description:</u> If you still want to prepare this kind of bid while using Scrum you should consider the following steps: developing a project vision and creating a prospect for your statement values. After that, you should create a product backlog with both functional and nonfunctional items so you can have full system characteristics. The next steps are inserting and prioritizing the product backlog while doing revisions and reviews with the customer's feedback on your value statements.

After this first part is done then you have to create the amount of design and architecture that is necessary for product development estimation. All these estimates and other scalable factors have to be described in the part of the bid named ''Release plan''. That part needs to contain your discussion of prospect values and increments that will be delivered. Try to introduce changes in product backlog content and priorities and base your whole bid around the product backlog concept. Using these processes your bid will be not only complete but educational for those who are not familiar with agile practices and concept of iterations and reprioritization of functionalities.

Activity 9: Project funding

The person responsible: Product owner

Purpose: The first Scrum phase and all previous activities if done correctly can now be presented to the potential investor, company, or some other kind of funding source. By the time that the first phase gets to this activity, the majority of the details have been determined so the Product owner can present a very clear and achievable plan. The purpose of the project has to be justified, and at the same time Product owner has to convince potential investors that supporting the project is the right thing to do. One part of the Product owner's responsibility during this activity is to construct presentable ROI and uses it to demonstrate deliverable benefits in comparison to costs. This way the funding source can have a good overview of their investment and their gain.

Assumptions: Potential investors will believe that the project is manageable and targeted technology available. It is assumed that all plans will be implemented without any bigger issues through the use of sprints and other techniques that Scrum offers. Additionally, it is possible that at one point project management will have to provide some education on agile processes as a part of their plan presentation.

Risks: Greatest risks for users of agile practices, in general, are with strictly hierarchical institutions or organizations such as the Department of Defense procurement for example.

In agile practices ROI measurements are lent and many activities are not completely defined in the first Scrum phase. This is why hierarchical environments sometimes aren't the right choice for funding Scrum projects.

<u>Description:</u> Investor or funding source expects immediate reports on successfully delivered working functionality. Keep in mind that funding is mostly provided because the investor expects great benefits and return on investment that will be adequate to the vision he supported. All of the funding sources want to have progress measurements, mechanisms for tracking and reporting project status and eventually report about the successful implementation of the product release.

Conclusion

Agile practices need development teams that can build working functionalities and deliver their increments at the end of every sprint or iteration. There are some processes such as Extreme Programming and Scrum that require that each of these increments has to be potentially shippable to the users. The usual procedure is that this increment is made of code lines that were tested several times and built to work as a fully executable and functional and documented feature. This documentation can be found either in user documentation or in Help files of the increment.

If more exact use has been created for the product's increment during any particular spring, it is documented as an additional product feature thus standardized as one.

By the end of 1990, many practices in software development have promoted formal models, formal communication, using document templates and computer tools that are optimized and standardized depending on the need. Scrum is based on face to face communication and if the Scrum Master is unable to communicate with the team this way, the probability of misunderstanding is introduced.

Scrum suggests that whenever a team member tries to formulate ideas the best way is to write them down and try to turn them into the most understandable version. The person who listens needs to be able to understand the expectations of the presenter within its own context of experience. The aim of Scrum isn't to have the most detailed plan which everyone will follow blindly. The goal is to maximize communication between those who are involved with the project and therefore increase their productivity.

Communication can be maximized through different techniques and tools that will guide team members while they are focused on writing the code. In this case, the models are not there for the documentation but for the sake of the thought process. Teams are collocated so that each member can communicate face to face and try to find a solution in case any problem emerges. If the team is collocated in the open space it will strengthen the bond between the teammates. It is also more effective because you don't have to go from office to office just to ask a question. Face to face communication in Scrum provided better results and sometimes hyper productivity because the whole development team could connect on a deeper level, see how other members feel and act while creating a more comfortable and more relaxed working environment.

Scrum is considered to be one of the revolutionary approaches because it was the first method that used iterations. In Scrum, these iterations are thirty day-long sprints as we already learned through the book. The practice showed that iterations limited to no more than thirty days help the team to effectively solve problems while staying focused on the requirements that need to be delivered.

It is recommended that these development teams have no more than seven members if possible. According to experienced Scrum masters, seven is the most optimal number of people that can form a strong mental bond and share common system values and ideas and all that while writing the code together. Smaller teams minimize the chance of misunderstanding and are easier to point in the right direction.

In Scrum, it is desirable to have a shared code library. If the team makes rigorous code standards and everyone in the team is ready to accept those standards and read everything carefully, every team member will understand the system and the code. Scrum minimized the amount of documentation written code literally becomes the design of the system which is why the code should be easy to read.

Many practices would rather reduce team support and their productivity than give up the goals that need to be achieved. Scrum tends to find a way to intelligently implements different phases of project management. This is why one of Scrum's real goals is to find a balance rather than cut out team productivity. On the contrary, Scrum has a way to achieve maximal team productivity during the project development process.

In the last ten chapters, we could see why agile practices are becoming more popular in the last decades and what their possibilities are. There is a clear distinction between traditional approaches and agile methods with Scrum as their main representative. Scrum is considered to be one of the original agile methodologies and it proved its successful implementation on multiple levels. Nowadays, large numbers of organizations use Scrum principles in their project development. Scrum was the first methodology used in software development processes that introduced the concept of self-organization. It was the first time in which developers had to figure out what to do instead of just following already determined tasks. The benefits of Scrum are countless. But most importantly, Scrum creates an enjoyable working environment that leads to happier and more creative individuals that will give their best efforts to deliver the best possible result in the shortest time frame.

Resources

Harold, E. (1992). Crystal healing. Ringwood, Vic.: Viking.

Images: 1 million Stunning Free Images to Use Anywhere - Pixabay. (n.d.). Retrieved from https://pixabay.com/